JAMES BOND, ROUTE 9, AND ME

Frieda Toth

JAMES BOND, ROUTE 9, AND ME

Frieda Toth

ISBN:978-0-970-1664-6-3

©2023 Frieda Toth
All Rights Reserved

No part of this book may be reproduced, or stored in a retrieval system, or transmitted in any form or by any means, electronic, mechanical, photocopying, recording, or otherwise, without express written permission of the publisher.

Published by Warren History Press
Warren County Historical Society 50
Gurney Lane
Queensbury, NY 12804
www.wcnyhs.org
mail@wcnyhs.org

Table of Contents

Introduction, 1

Chapter 1
Recreating A Historical Trip, 2

A Bit on Bond, 2
Summary of The Spy Who Loved Me and Background, 3
Preparing: Getting the Vespa, Planning the Time, 7
Recon by Car and A Week of Strategizing, 12
Let's Take It from the Top (of NYS), 14

Chapter 2
The Beautiful Adirondacks, 19

Adirondacks As In the Book, 19
My Adirondacks, 20
]Brief History of the Adirondacks, 21

Chapter 3
Sights Ian Probably Missed
What impressed me in the Adirondacks, From the North to the South, 25

Ausable Chasm, 25
Underground Railroad Museum, 28
Shamrock Inn, 29
Ausable Marsh, 31
Sculpture Garden, 32
Keeseville, 32
Trail Heads, 34
Prospect Mt. Trail, 36
Adirondack History Museum, 38
Elizabethtown, 45
Frontier Town, 51
Schroon Lake, 52
Pottersville, 53
Natural Stone Bridge and Caves, 54
Warrensburg, 56

Chapter 4
Lake George Area
Sights Ian Probably Really Saw, 58

Storytown, U.S.A., 58
Wiawaka, 59
Lake George Village, 69
The Cruise, 73
Fort William Henry, 84

Chapter 5
People I Met, 93

Chapter 6
Challenges, Challenges, 101

The Challenges of Packing , 104

Chapter 7
Coming Home, 106

Acknowledgements, 110

Index Words, People, Whatever, 110

Sources
On Line
Ephemera

Introduction

In King's Cross Station, London, there's a half of a luggage cart, handle side out, sticking out of a brick wall, and thousands of people every year get their photographs taken with it. Near the half luggage cart is a sign that reads "Platform 9 3/4," a reference to the fantasy world of Harry Potter. People are delighted to have their picture taken with Platform 9 3/4 and imagine themselves going to Hogwart's, or at least, with this photo, feel close to the Potterverse.

That's how it is for people who love certain books and authors. After a while, rereading them isn't enough. You start to collect memorabilia, or even to go on pilgrimages. There are popular museums for Anne of Green Gables and Laura Ingalls Wilder, and people stood outside 221B Baker Street in London for so long that eventually, the locals yielded to public pressure and put a Sherlock Holmes museum there, even though at the time, Sir Arthur Conan Doyle was writing the address didn't exist.

This feeling, this need to get closer to the author or to the stories, is what happened to me with Ian Fleming, who, of course, created the world's most famous spy, James Bond. His stories have been translated into twenty languages and are the basis for the world's longest- running movie franchise. Few people know that Bond, the jet-setting man of action, had an adventure in the Adirondacks in northern New York State. The book in which this happens is The Spy Who Loved Me.

It was a desire to feel closer to the world of Bond that led me to trace the route of a Bond Girl, on a motor scooter going only thirty-five miles an hour, down Route 9 through the beautiful Adirondacks. On my six-day journey, I revisited sites Ian Fleming mentioned, noting where time had stood still and where it had marched on, and I had thrills of my own. Timeline

Sun. Aug 1, recon Mon. Aug. 2, recon Tuesday-Thursday, normal work week Friday, Aug. 6, 6 am–trip begins! Friday, during day, reach Canadian border, take pictures, turn around Friday, sleep at the Shamrock Inn Saturday, wake and explore the land of Ausable Saturday night, camp by the Boquet River Sunday morning, continue south Sunday evening, sleep at Wiawaka, Lake George Monday morning, explore Lake George Monday afternoon, go home Following Saturday, re-explore Lake George August 21, sadly return scooter

Chapter 1
Recreating A Historic Trip

A Bit on Bond

Now that the twenty-five Bond films have thrilled audiences for over sixty years, making Bond the most successful fictional character in two separate centuries, it's easy to forget that James Bond began as a literary character. Indeed, some people don't forget; some people never even knew. There are twelve original full-length Bond thrillers and two collections of short stories. As with any book adaptation, The Spy Who Loved Me, Pan edition with map cover the movies took liberties in adapting stories to film, but after a while they simply ran out of books to adapt and gave Bond new storylines. There are now over twice as many James Bond movies as original James Bond books.

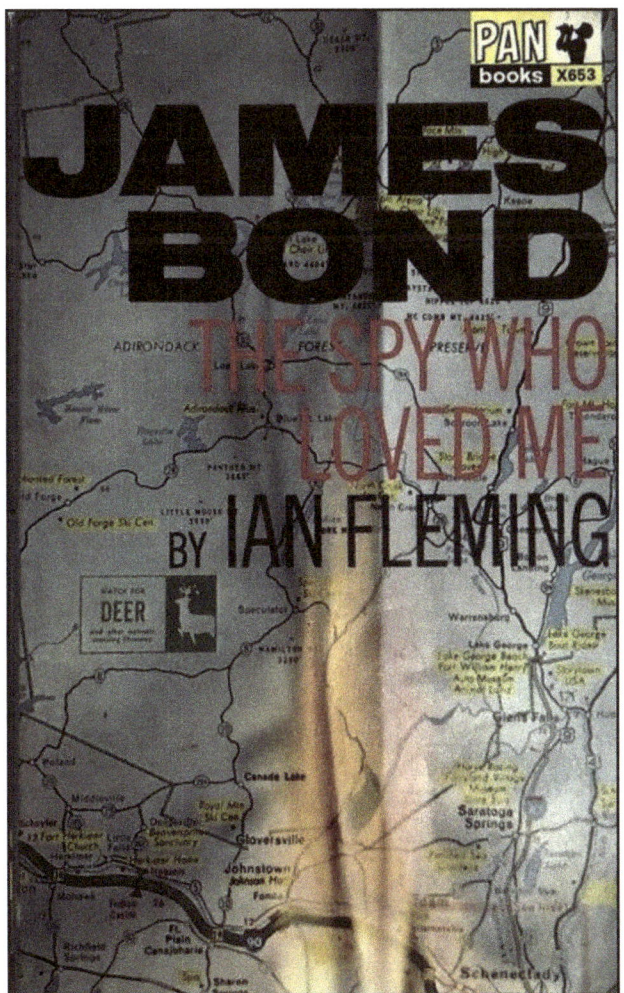

The Spy Who Loved Me, Pan edition with map cover

In addition to changes made to the Bond character that were necessary for film, there were some changes that perhaps were not necessary, but when they happened changed, the perception of Bond. In the United States, we associate Bond with exotic, often tropical locations, but one-third of Bond books feature important scenes in the United States, and two of the books have scenes in northern New York. Diamonds Are Forever, in book form, has scenes at the track in Saratoga Springs, around the town, and in a local bath house. When these scenes were left out of the movie, it markedly changed the perception of Bond, but the Bond films are Hollywood -- made in America--and American sites are not as exotic to an American eye. Literary Bond is very familiar with American cities of New York, Las Vegas, New Orleans, and Chicago, and, when Ian Fleming wrote a nonfiction book called Thrilling Cities, a dozen

American cities were included. There's a famous bit of advice, "write what you know," and Fleming knew the United States, particularly the East coast, well. His intelligence work (yes, he really was a spy, sort of) meant he had work to do that took him from Montreal to New York City to Washington, and he was frequently in New York. In fact, he had an office in what we call The Rock, 30 Rockefeller Center. Fleming also lived and worked in Washington, D.C. for a time, sharing a "flat" with fellow British Intelligence agent and future writer Roald Dahl.

Dahl and Fleming were both tall, dashing, and known to be heartbreakers. They even dated the same woman while in D.C. Millicent Rogers, who unwittingly lent her name to a minor character in that Bond novel that takes place in New York State, The Spy Who Loved Me, in fact, the book whose path I retraced. (Dahl and Fleming each went on to marry a beautiful, sophisticated woman and each was a terrible, unfaithful husband. But what did you expect?) Fleming had been to New York with some frequency before his intelligence work, visiting both as a stockbroker as early as 1937 (he was admittedly awful at this) and as a journalist (he was excellent at that). Fleming was able to finagle his contract at the Sunday Times so as to give himself two months off a year, which he used to write, while in Jamaica. Yes, you read that right. Two months off.

We often associate Bond with Jamaica, and both Bond and his creator spent a good deal of time there. Fleming had a house, Goldeneye, which he bought with an ex-girlfriend's money and on which he built a house you can still visit, if you have the resources. However, every time he went to and from Jamaica he stopped in New York for a few days or weeks. He had favorite hotels (which he lauded in Thrilling Cities), some of which still stand, but more often than not he stayed with his friend Ivar Bryce in his house on 161st Street. Bryce said in his memoirs that Fleming knew the New York music scene better than he did, and told about a time Fleming strong-armed him into going to listen to some young Italian singer that Fleming thought had promise. The "young Italian" was Frank Sinatra. Every summer for about ten years, Fleming would visit the track at Saratoga, staying at one of Bryce's other houses, Black Hole Hollow Farm, which is in Cambridge, New York, on the border of Vermont. So it is easy to see that he could write about New York with more than passing familiarity. He once said, "I've examined the area fairly thoroughly . . . it all helps to build up reality in my books." All this is to say that Bond has a firm presence in the United States, and I really should not have been surprised to find out that The Spy Who Loved Me was set in New York State.

Summary of The Spy Who Lived Me and Background

If you are trying to re-create an event that happened years ago or a fictional event set in the past, chances are you are going to have to compromise here and there. Fans of the old PBS series

1900 House will remember times when the materials the Bowler family sought were simply not available, or when the producers found that the 1900 way of doing something was so dangerous that it was illegal at the time of filming. So it was with my own trip - some things I could copy exactly, some things I had to skip or compromise on if I wanted to make the trip at all.

The Spy Who Loved Me, written in 1960, takes place in 1961, and was published in 1962, three years before I was born. While we are sixty years past the action now, I was around and cognizant of my surroundings close enough to when the book happened that recreating it is largely memory, with some research.

The story opens with a young woman, Vivienne, sitting in a cabin in the Adirondacks, reflecting on how she came to be there. She is young, naive, but she has a zest for life. She tells her story of growing up in Canada, an orphan in the care of a caring but emotionally distant aunt, going to finishing school in England, then finding a career in newspapers, but she suffers crippling heartache that sends her back to North America to regroup. She decides to get a Vespa and motor down the East coast in search of adventure, and, eventually, she hopes for another newspaper job. But when we find her, she is in a cabin, off-season in the Adirondacks, where gangsters later muscle their way in and would have murdered her in an insurance scam were it not for the timely arrival of James Bond.

If you think this would make a great movie, I agree – so why does the movie of that name take place far from New York? Ian Fleming was displeased, even embarrassed, by some of the negative reviews of this book, the only one where he tried to write from a woman's point of view. He was so embarrassed that he stopped the paperback production in England (although not in the United States) and ordered that only the title, not its plot, could be used for a film.

After many years enjoying Bond, I wanted to see if such a trip were possible. Frankly, it sounded like a lot of fun, and, having grown up just outside Adirondack Park, the trip seemed plausible. This trip was also the perfect project for a COVID-infected and socially distanced world: mostly outside, and mostly solo.

Sometimes people ask me how I got involved in the world of James Bond in the first place. It's a valid question, since movie Bond seems counter to all people know about me: I am feminist, not that interested in worldly goods, and tend to prefer books of history to action movies. But in my teenage years, my then boyfriend introduced me to Bond movies, which led me to getting the books from the library where I worked, and then to reading The Spy Who Loved Me.

That's how I remembered it, and told it, for years. In my teen years, VCRs were so new that Blockbuster would rent VCRs along with videotapes, because the machines were so costly as to be beyond the reach of most families. Libraries were only just beginning to have tapes to borrow, and they were costly enough that you would only own your favorites. The first James Bond movie I saw was probably Live and Let Die, and I remember my boyfriend apologizing, "Most Bond movies begin with a naked woman dancing in silhouette. It's just what happens. It has nothing to do with the movie."

I loved the movie and most of the next few we watched, although I remember cringing at the sexual assault committed by Sean Connery, particularly in Thunderball and Goldfinger. Still, I liked the Bond character pretty well, I loved the locations, the thrills, the mystery, and I started to borrow the books from the library where I worked, where I work now. I didn't get the books in any particular order. I had grown up on Nancy Drew, Hardy Boys, Alfred Hitchcock's The Three Investigators, and on Meg mysteries, which don't have to be read in order, and I had no notion that Bond books had an overarching timeline. Looking back, I wish I had known, and that I had read them in publication order, because the character would have made more sense.

Anyway, for years, I had been saying to my friends, puzzled about my Bond obsession, and to the groups that paid me to talk about Ian Fleming, that my high school sweetheart was responsible for my interest in him. But now I am not so sure. You see, YouTube has made old television shows readily available, and I have enjoyed going back over all the things we watched as a family in the 1960s and 1970s. Before cable, everything that was on TV before nine in the evening had to be considered suitable for families. That meant either outright wholesome fare such as The Waltons or shows where the double and triple entendres were hidden in complicated vocabulary words, such as with The Smothers Brothers.

One day, while scrolling through my old childhood favorites, the show Get Smart appeared, and memories came flooding back to me. Get Smart was a parody of spy movies, starring Don Adams as the spy, and Barbara Feldon as his assistant, called "Ninety-Nine." Of course, I was young, so I did not know it was a parody.

I was fascinated by the Cone of Silence and the shoe phone which were nods to Bond gadgets. And I was terrified when Maxwell Smart appeared to be in danger. I particularly remember one episode with a sinister villain who had poisoned fingernails, and it looked as though it was all over for Max until he said, "The mosquito, Ninety-Nine." My childish heart leapt at the knowledge that Maxwell Smart was surely saved; the villain, being bitten by the mosquito, would poison himself scratching with those terrible fingernails. I could foresee this before it happened and, as an adult, I think this young realization triggered some kind of love of suspense and a good ending.

In any case, I have been saying for years, and I meant it, that my husband is responsible for my love of James Bond, and he certainly introduced me to the Bond world. But would I have taken to Bond had I not had a latent love of the spy genre, of gadgets and fast cars? The world will never know. There's a question sometimes asked on Twitter and Facebook: What book do you wish you could read again for the first time? Absolutely, The Spy Who Loved Me. When first reading this book, I had already enjoyed a number of Fleming's thrillers, and had in these books been whisked away to Istanbul, to Paris, to Moscow. And, while I sat on the shore of Lake George, it leapt from the page at me: "I had come all the way from London to . . .Lake George, the famous American tourist resort in the Adirondacks - that vast expanse of mountains, lakes and pine forests that forms most of the northern territory of New York State." I remember that I actually closed the book and reopened it to read again. I was that surprised to see Bond in my home area.

I grew up and out of Bond, but thirty years or so after I first read he had been in Lake George, I revisited the book, which mentions Lake George and Glens Falls each over a dozen times; Albany several times; the Hudson River; and even Mechanicville. I was impressed that Fleming spelled both Glens Falls and Mechanicville correctly, and even more impressed that he correctly identified the sordid happenings of our famous, tiny bad part of town, the South Street area.

The whole book is worth it for me when I show my local friends that passage. Millicent is annoyed at her husband, Jed, who is putting his hands all over Viv, the main character. Millicent and Jed are on their way to Glens Falls, and Millicent tries to get Jed to knock off the harassment by saying, "Come on Jed, you can work off those urges on West Street tonight." Locals know South Street as the area of ill repute; Broad Street, which crosses it, was called "West Street" in the 1960s and did indeed have that reputation. Some old timers would nod at me when I mentioned Fleming had local connections, and they would hint at inside information of the most tantalizing meager kind. "Yes, my Uncle Chet knew Fleming, but I don't remember anything else because he died when I was eight." "My father used to give some weird English man a ride home sometimes. Later I saw his name on theater marquees, but nobody believed me." "Yes, he was here, he used to stay in Fort Edward. That's all I know." "He used the library in Bolton Landing sometimes. No, I don't know any more. I wasn't paying attention to my grandfather because I was in second grade." Some locals knew, but most people were surprised, or even incredulous, when I told them that Ian Fleming, creator of James Bond, had ever been in the area. I became so eager to share the information that the great Ian Fleming set a book in my hometown area that I wrote an article about Ian Fleming's connections to the north country for Voices (the journal of the New York Folklore Society). I then breathed a sigh of relief that I had gotten that off my chest. I thought I'd never have to think about it again, but one day I got a Facebook message from a man claiming to be a London editor and agent, who wanted me to write for him. I didn't believe him and closed the Facebook window while looking him up in another. He was who he said he was, so I began writing articles for him and his online magazine, "Artistic License Renewed." This led to a Twitter presence, a good side gig of presenting lectures on Ian Fleming in the United States and puzzled indulgent looks from all my friends who had to listen to my James Bond obsessions. None was surprised when I told them I was going to reenact part of a book.

Preparing: Getting the Vespa, Planning the Time

Our heroine, Viv Michel, was equipped with a brand-new Vespa, and all the stuff that would have made such a trip comfortable in 1960: fur lined goggles, saddle bags, nice leather boots, a jacket and gloves. It is no accident, in a James Bond book, that her get-up has a vague feel of the kind of activities featured in the popular book Fifty Shades of Grey. Well, fur-lined goggles are no longer easy to find, and my scooter didn't have room for saddlebags. I had to 'make do' on the costume with a leather jacket.

I didn't have any idea where to find a 1960s era Vespa. I knew I couldn't afford to buy one, even if I found such a thing, but it was important to me that I do the trip on a motor scooter, not in a car. I might possibly have compromised by using a motorcycle, but I didn't happen to own one.

I wish I had an interesting story about finding the motor scooter, but this was accomplished as easily as mentioning to a friend that I was going to try to rent one for a trip. "Oh, let me ask my dad. He has a scooter he is not using." Her dad didn't even charge me for the use of it! The only things he wanted were for me to have a good time, and to not mention him by name in the stories he knew I'd tell later, so I will call him by the name of "Len." And what a thing of beauty it was! A 2008 Honda Metropolitan, white with vivid blue trim, squooshy black seat with about a gallon of storage under it, and, in lieu of saddle bags, a matching blue vintage milk crate on the back. It may not have been strictly period, but when, on the trail, people asked me how old my scooter was, I knew my friend had made the right choice for me.

The slow speed of the Honda scooter turned out to be an unexpected blessing. As I have mentioned, upon learning I was making this crazy trip, a biker friend offered to keep me company, which is to say, he didn't want me to make this trip alone. But that is the entire point, that the protagonist of The Spy Who Loved Me was making this joyous adventure on her own, to escape her sad past and be independent. I knew that telling my friend he was missing the point would seem ungrateful, so I told him a different part of the truth, "This thing goes thirty five miles an hour, and you ride a Harley. You would not enjoy this." He did not press further, so I got my solo trip.

Once promised the scooter, getting hold of it was another matter. This scooter had not been used in years, although Len, the owner, was pretty sure it was in good working condition and just needed an inspection sticker. He arranged for it to be dropped off at Sportline in Queensbury, NY, not far from my house, for the inspection.

It didn't pass. It wouldn't even start.

July, in the Adirondacks, is not the best time to ask for repairs on a bike or motor scooter. Too many people need the work done, and there is a long list of people getting such work done starting as early as May, so Len and I had to just hope he had dropped it off in time. One week before the planned trip, after several pleading calls from Len had not yielded a bike, I went in with my copy of The Spy Who Loved Me, to impress upon the staff how important it was that this be done. I showed the mechanics the book with the map of the Adirondacks on it, and one said, "Fleming? Someone named Fleming wrote James Bond? My name is Fleming!" And the other said, "Is this the scooter order? We just finished that." I wasn't sorry I made the trip because I enjoyed the conversation, but it turns out it was not necessary.

I did have to figure out how to get the scooter home. I had driven to ask them to fix the thing, but it was too big to fit in my car. I don't have a truck, and the people who had dropped off the scooter were busy that week. Not having a lot of time to spare, it seemed the best thing for me to do was to drive home and return on my roller blades.

I roller-bladed from my house in Glens Falls to Sportline in Queensbury the next morning, happily making most of the trip on a quiet, tree-lined street and just hitting the traffic about a third of a mile from the motorcycle place.

"I'm here for the scooter," I said to the mechanics at the counter, different people from before.

"Wait, are you the one that just zipped here on roller blades?" "Yes, that's me," I said, anticipating what would come next. "I bet that gave you a laugh; I'm used to being the town character." "No, No, we're not laughing at all. That was amazing! No one's ever picked up a bike that way before." He paused. "Are you familiar with two wheels?" "I have my motorcycle license, but I have never ridden this before. Can you show me everything?" The mechanic patiently showed me how to open the seat for storage, how to apply the parking brake, and, so importantly, where to fill the gas tank. I never would have found that on my own because this was under where I put my feet, and under a mat as well. He made me rehearse starting it, the turn signals, and parking it before he let me be on my way, and I am grateful for that.

To park it, the entire scooter had to be moved, because rather than resting on one side, as a bicycle does, the thing rests on a cradle on a hinge. It took more strength than I would have thought to put this into position, but getting it off the cradle was easy. Once the mechanic was satisfied I knew what I was doing, I threw my roller blades in the milk crate on the back and started for home.

As soon as I was on the scooter, I felt exhilaration. I still took a back route home, worrying that I might crash this borrowed marvel. You see, I don't actually own a motorcycle. After I took the weekend course in motorcycle safety on a borrowed purple Kawasaki I just never got around to buying a bike. I'm a homeowner and a parent and there always seemed to be a better use for the money. That the nice man who lent me his scooter knew this about me and let me have the Honda anyway will always make me very grateful, but the enormity of his generosity left me trembling.

A map like Viv had on her trip

I didn't want to spend over three hundred miles round trip uneasy, so after I got the scooter safely home, I carved out time to take it out on the road, early in the morning so as to avoid traffic.

The first time I took it out, really took it out, I was up at sunrise and determined to practice stopping and signaling. I'd ridden the thing home without hitting a light, merely slowing down instead of stopping. This was somewhat unnerving because the idle was so slow that it always felt as though the machine were about to stall, but after a fifteen minute ride around my neighborhood, it felt better.

The scooter's small size was difficult for me. It had a motor, and signal lights, and went fast enough that it was road legal, but it was so light in weight that I kept forgetting to use the signal lights, using the hand signals I use while biking. It took several trips out before I was really comfortable with the signal lights.

As I got better at driving, and spent longer times on trips, I realized I would need real motorcycle gloves. Even at thirty miles an hour, in the early morning, my hands were becoming cold and stiff. I went back to Sportline, where the gloves that seemed to offer real protection were all too big for my hands. I asked the clerk, "Do you have anything for women?" He said, "Women's gloves are just like men's gloves, only pink and more expensive. But if you want something smaller, we've got that. You've got the blue scooter, right? Let me see if I have blue gloves in the back." I might add that one of the reasons I love Sportline is that the staff there are not only helpful, but they also seem happy to be there.

Before I had my real trip, I had gotten my rides around the neighborhood up to about an hour at a time, but still I was nervous. I expected to be on the road for twelve hours, minus bathroom and snack breaks. One hour was very little practice, but it was what I had time for. The morn-

A map like Viv had on her triping I started out, I was feeling equal amounts of joy that I was really, finally, doing this, and trepidation. "This thing is worth six thousand dollars. Don't crash. Don't crash," I muttered as I took off. But soon the exhilaration of the trip finally becoming real overcame my doubts and I was flying, if not in reality, not in velocity, at least in my feelings.

Viv's equipment included a map from Esso, the old gas station chain. I was not sure why she needed such a map, because she simply headed down Route 9 from the Canadian border until she got to Lake George.

Ready to take to the road After I obtained a copy of this map from E-Bay, however, it made more sense. The Esso map listed tourist attractions, and, of course, gas stations, something both she and I would need. The scooter got one hundred miles to the gallon, and that sounds like a lot, but it is one hundred and seventy-four miles from my house in Glens Falls to the Canadian border, and the gas tank was not even a full gallon.

Ready to take to the road

OK, scooter, map, clothing. Clothing! The storage in the scooter was very small. Viv, whose Vespa came with saddlebags, had plenty of room for clothing. Just the same, I read the book and re-read it searching for the part about how she did laundry. I never found such a section, making me wonder what I would do. I considered wearing a backpack with extra clothes but came to believe that twelve hours on a scooter carrying a backpack would be too much for me over the days the trip would take. And then, I knew that sometimes I would be parked somewhere, in a lot, not in a hotel. I didn't want to have to be looking after a pack. OK, everything would have to go in the small storage of the scooter under the seat, or in the milk crate that the owner had affixed to the back.

Luckily, I like to pack light, ever since my college days, and have become accustomed to rinsing out underwear in hotel rooms. I'd need only one change of clothing, plus a bathing suit, plus the layers necessary for the chill I was likely to experience in the Adirondack nights. Easy. I have clothes for the cold, because I live here.

Picking the time for the trip, by the way, had been relatively simple. Viv says her misadventures happened in October, but as a lifelong resident of the Adirondack area, I can tell you that the atmosphere she describes is unmistakably that of an Adirondack August. The storms, the warm sunshine, the busy tourist traps and liveliness which Viv calls "honky tonk" are all Northern New York summer. Ian Fleming was known to go to the horse racing track in Saratoga for many years, and horse racing is an August occurrence, or at least was, before the season was extended in 2010. It was a relief to know that Viv described Adirondack August, because my child goes to summer camp at that time, and would therefore neither need care nor miss me while I was gone.

Alas, 2021 was the summer of rain in northern New York. July 2021 had so much rain I didn't dare make hotel reservations. I didn't know, even as I saved money and collected donations from sponsors who believed in me, whether I'd have to put the trip off a year, either because of bad weather or because of changing COVID restrictions. After I borrowed the scooter and practiced on it between rainstorms, I still didn't know if the trip would happen.

Another obstacle was the fact that I was starting from Viv's ending point: instead of motoring down the route, I had to drive up to the border, turn around, and come back. I tried to get the scooter shipped to the border without me, and then to rent a truck to drive the scooter up (and drop off the truck). but neither of these solutions ended up being viable. So, I realized I would have to drive the scooter round trip, taking notes and pictures each way.

Recon by Car and a Week of Strategizing

It stopped raining just about when I dropped my daughter off at camp. At that time I did a recon, by car. You may wonder why I would do a reconnaissance in a place I have lived most of my life, but although I know the Adirondacks well, I had never traversed them by scooter or motorcycle, and I took a car recon to make sure things were safe for the trip. I needed not only to know the location of every gas station. I needed to see, ahead of time, where traffic would likely be heavy, and the drivers might be hostile to a scooter driver.

If you've never ridden a bike on back roads, you may wonder why I was so worried about hostility, but it was my own experience that made me apprehensive. As a bike rider, and as a rollerblader, I am conscientious, sticking to my own lane and observing traffic laws, but I have had drivers try to run me off the road, have had horrible things shouted at me, have even had things thrown at me, so I take the bike trail rather than the road when I can. On a scooter, smaller than a motorcycle, would the drivers of cars treat me the way they treated cyclists?

Most importantly, I needed to find several places to rest my head on the real trip.

The Adirondacks tourist season, even in year two of COVID, was quite a bit busier than it had been in 1960, and there are far fewer cabins. I wanted, as much as possible, to stay at places that had been open when Viv would have made her trip, and such places don't always have websites, even in 2021. It would be necessary to visit them in person to make a reservation. I had, online, found one place to stay (not a historical location), right on Route 9, halfway to Canada, for the recon, so I planned to take pictures, find out where gas stations and eateries were, and generally make sure the route was safe for me, one week ahead of the planned trek.

The week in between the recon and the actual trip was a cheerful frenzy of packing and repacking. As precious as my space was, I still made room to pack orange and green tomatoes (firm for travel) and zucchini from my garden as host gifts. I packed a couple of tiny paperbacks. I found quick drying clothing which I could rinse out nightly, and those good sturdy motorcycle gloves. I realized with relief that the bulkiest thing on the trip, my leather jacket, would be on my back. Then I remembered I had to find a tent small enough to pack.

Food was going to be a challenge, I knew. In the book, Viv subsists mostly on bacon sandwiches, fruit, and coffee. I like bacon as well as anybody, and possibly when I was in my twenties this would have seemed like a good plan, but I am in my mid-fifties, and can no longer subsist on empty calories and enthusiasm. In addition to vegetables from my garden, I got

A map of part of Viv's journey

plums from the Farmers' Market, and some granola bars. I figured that on the way I could get meals, but for snacks I would have something good for me. The food bag, with other things I expected to need handy such as bug spray and the registration for the scooter, I put under the seat. Clothing would go in the milk crate. A plastic milk crate isn't, strictly speaking, 1960s period equipment, but it was a pretty blue to match the paint of the machine and bore the label "Dobert's Dairy." Dobert's was founded in 1931 in Glens Falls and was around in the 1960s when Viv would have been on her trip, even if it was not in the book.

My jacket was not, technically, a motorcycle jacket. It fell too long, and the pockets did not zip, which made me worry that things would fall out as I rode. Still, it was real leather, a gift from a friend, and as real motorcycle jackets are costly, it would have to do. (I had been embarrassed to accept this jacket from my friend, because it was too big for me, and I was disinclined to bring that up to someone giving me a gift. Luckily, I guess luckily, I suppose luckily, menopause gave me the extra bulk so this jacket fits perfectly now, and anyone who wants to tell me it was indolence, not meno- A map of part of Viv's journey pause, that caused the weight gain is welcome to join me at my pole dancing class).

Because I was terrified my wallet would fall out of those pockets, I got a pouch to hang on a string around my neck, and in the pouch went the wallet and the phone. Well, most of the time the phone was in the pouch. Sometimes, it would be mounted on the handlebars so I could film the road as I was on it. I found a pretty sturdy phone holder for this, but it turned out the one I chose didn't correct for road vibrations, so filming while riding turned out not to be practical. However, stills from the road turned out great.

By the time I "started" my trip, that is to say copying the one in the book, I had been back and forth on the route one and a half times. First, I did it by car, then I had to go back and drive up on the scooter, and "start" the trip as the character did. This makes the narrative a bit confusing.

Let's Take It from the Top (of NYS)

Have you ever ridden a motor scooter? I had not, before I decided to take one for a three hundred-mile, four-day round trip. A scooter rides something between a motorcycle and a bike, but with characteristics unique to a scooter. For both a bike and a motorcycle, you are astride as for a horse. For a scooter, there is nothing between your legs, and the sensation is that of motoring along on a very fast-wheeled office chair.

In both the case of a motorcycle and a scooter, the right hand controls the acceleration, leaving the left free to signal, either manually or with the controls on the handlebars. Both hands control the brakes, and, as on a bicycle, most of us use one brake more than the other. I find a scooter much more stable than most motorcycles, and certainly more stable than a bike, but the lightness of the scooter made me feel more like I was on a bike, and vulnerable, than on the powerful machine that is a Kawasaki or a Harley.

A scooter makes a pleasant buzzing sound, and I am told that "Vespa" is Italian for "wasp" because the buzzing is so insect-like. But the quiet is also a little dangerous! Harleys are famous for their obnoxious noise, but this sound allows drivers of cars to be aware of Harleys long before the drivers may see them. The pleasant buzz of the scooter made me terribly anxious that the other drivers would not see me or hear me, and might hit me. A road-legal scooter or motorbike, in contrast to a bicycle, must, by law, be IN the road, not on the shoulder. So, before I even began the trip, I knew that in order to be safe, I would have to

At the Canadian border ready to start my journey

The border crossing into Canada

hit any urban areas at low traffic times, and that if anybody was tailgating me, I would have to pull over and let them pass. Not that there are a great many "urban areas" in the Adirondacks, but when you are on a scooter, two or three cars coming at you or around you constitute heavy traffic, it only takes one aggressive driver to be deadly.

In reality, I traveled up and down Route 9, several times, but for ease of storytelling, and because Viv's narrative starts pretty much at the border between Canada and New York State, that's where I'll begin this travelogue, after the wobbly thrill of driving three hundred miles north.

Have you ever felt elation and relief at the same time? That was me, at the Canadian border. I DID it! I had ridden the scooter almost two hundred miles in a day and was at the crossing to Canada. I did the trip! I didn't crash the borrowed scooter!

I could not cross the border, as COVID kept it closed. Even if I had been permitted to enter Canada, I could not have done so at that location. Route 9 no longer is a valid entry point to Canada. Since I-87 is literally a few feet away, the Route 9 entry was closed some time ago in favor of entry by the highway, but the scooter is not road safe for highway driving. I could only look at the customs houses and dream.

North Country apples

At the Canadian border ready to start my journey

The area had the air of a dystopian movie set. Nothing but concrete and concrete and concrete in several directions as far as the eye could see. No trees broke up the grey landscape, and the only color was the dulling green of the highway signs. What a contrast to the charming town I

Snowplow tun around signs are in abundance in the North Country

had come through to get there. I took some happy selfies and headed back to town.

I could not get even close to the customs house on Route 9 or the highway but thought I might have better luck at Rouse's Point, a small town nearby. I The border crossing into Canada remember in college having a friend who lived there, who said that the border crossing officers got so used to the local children, and they would let them cross the bridge on their bikes all day if they wanted. I didn't expect that kind of friendliness, but I thought I might at least get to talk to someone, maybe get a local story or two.

Here, I was disappointed. It wasn't that the guards would not talk to me. There were simply no guards. The building that guarded the border at Rouse's Point was empty, dark, and locked up. A huge orange plastic barrier stood hundreds of feet from the actual crossing, leaving no question that you were not going to get into Canada that day. I stopped at a local coffee shop, because people who sell coffee usually have the inside story, and asked if they knew when the border would be open. "No, we don't know anything. We're watching the papers," was the answer.

Rouse's Point, in contrast to the highway point of crossing, is green with trees, has beautiful old architecture, and an exquisite view of the lake. I hope I can come back in a few years and cross there.

Plattsburgh's most famous feature for years was its Air Force Base,

North Country apples closed in the fall of 1995. In 2007, the site was reopened as Plattsburgh International Airport. Just a little south of the town itself is a reminder of its former military importance in the form of a gleaming jet on display on Route 9. I was not that concerned with the former base, because it was not mentioned in The Spy Who Loved Me, but it seems to me that its absence from the book is an indication that Ian Fleming could not have spent much time there. Ian loved planes, loved to fly, loved to describe engines and the artistic lines of aircraft, and the character Viv had a love of engines and travel so it would have been natural for her to have enjoyed the base. A delightful site on the way south from Plattsburgh was The World's Largest MacIntosh Orchard, Chazy Orchard. It seems a funny thing to me, anyway, and emphasizes how hick our beloved North Country is - that this superlative is celebrated on the side of the barn and confirmed by Wikipedia. Also, the sight of this marvel reinforced the idea that Ian Fleming did not make this trip, himself, as research. If you read the James Bond novels, you will find that whatever Bond likes is the best/biggest/finest in the world. If Fleming, who loved apple pie, had been here, he would have mentioned the Biggest Orchard in the World. And I checked: this has been in existence for over one hundred years.

All over the North Country, but particularly in the small towns in the Adirondacks and other places north, are signs that we are accustomed to cold. Not only signs that we are accustomed to cold, but that we have pride in living with it. The winters here are so long that "snowplow turnaround" signs stay on roadsides year-round, as do signs that warn us about snowmobile

Snowplow turn around signs are in crossings. I took photos of these only

abundance in the North Country in Rouse's Point, but such signs were in multiple snowy towns, and even in August the cold doesn't feel that far away. It'll be cold again, soon enough.

People have asked me what it feels like to be on a scooter. It feels great. Wonderful, freeing, just slow enough not to worry that I'll break my neck, faster than I'd ever biked, wind on my face, control in my hands, just wonderful. It also felt validating. After years of having a motorcycle license, I finally went on the long trip I had dreamed of.

On the way back from the border, I stopped at a hot dog stand. I didn't know this when I stopped, but Clare and Carl's Texas Red Hots is a famous landmark. I pulled into the gravel parking lot only because I was intrigued by the

Clare and Carl's Texas Red Hots

building, which seemed to have such a tenuous connection to remaining upright. Clare and Carl's is a carhop establishment, and that made me smile, because there was no place to attach a tray on a scooter. Luckily, there were picnic tables. As it was a hot day, I parked in the shade on the opposite side of the building from the tables, which were in the sunshine but had umbrellas. A harried young man, built so as to make me think he came from Hollywood to play the part of "young, studly carhop" was literally running from table to car to restau- Clare and Carl's Texas Red Hots rant to keep up with the orders. I got the 'house special' with everything, which was delectable.

As hurried as he was, the carhop took the time to admire my scooter and offered to take my picture with it in front of the building. Having this man admire my bike, and my trek, and his wanting to preserve the memory for me was the perfect cap to having been to the border on the bike and to really feel as though I was having an adventure.

The hot dog was delicious, by the way. I don't know a lot about hot dog culture, so I was puzzled that at a place that called itself "Texas Red Hots" the special was a "Michigan Dog." Texas, Michigan, Chicago? What makes a hot dog belong to a geographical location? This was a good quality hot dog with meat sauce and finely chopped white onions. The roll was fresh and soft. I think most hot dog stands have their own recipe for meat sauce and I didn't even try to guess what was in it, but it was very good. The accompanying french fries were crisp, light, and plentiful.

Not far south from Clare and Carl's, I found myself in Adirondack Park.

Chapter 2

The Beautiful Adirondacks

Adirondack Park

Adirondacks, as In the Book

"That vast expanse of mountains, lakes, and pine forests which forms most of the northern territory of New York State." That's how Vivienne Michel, heroine of Ian Fleming's The Spy Who Loved Me, described the Adirondacks. Ian's character was writing in 1960, and this is still a pretty good description today. She went on to describe an Adirondack autumn, ". . . the real, wild maples flamed here and there like shrapnel-bursts," again a vivid and accurate picture. Those of us who live here may not always appreciate it, but world travelers say that the Adirondacks rank among the most beautiful locales in the world.

It must have been difficult for Ian Fleming to understand where he was. Yes, it is beautiful: acres and acres of mountains and lakes and streams, maintained trails, and lean-tos for camping. Scenic vistas year-round. But what, exactly, are the Adirondacks? How does "Adirondack" differ from any pretty part of Northern New York outside the "Adirondack" designation? It doesn't help that the word is used in so many ways. "Adirondack" can refer to the mountains themselves, the park, an architectural style-even to a style of chair.

My Adirondacks

I grew up just outside the Adirondacks, in Glens Falls, and while the borders of Adirondack Park are not arbitrary, the flora and fauna don't change just because they are outside the Blue Line, and I grew up in the company of chipmunks, whippoorwills, even the occasional moose on our property on the bank of the Hudson River. Technically, I am not an Adirondacker but it is hard not to feel like one when you're surrounded by hemlock.

As a child, I disliked whippoorwills. All night, most of the summer, they called and called and called. August nights were not easy sleeping for me. It was always too hot, and it stayed light far too late, and when the sun finally went down the constant calling of night birds was more than I could take. After I learned to count, I would count up to fifty repetitions of "Whip poor WILL!" before they would stop, and each time they got to the end I would think I could finally sleep, but a few minutes later they would start up again.

Pine trees are in abundance

Now, the many acres of woods where I grew up are taken over by little riverfront houses, and I could cry when I think how I resented the whippoorwill. If the 'Blue Line' that designated the Adirondack Park had extended just a little farther, the woods of my childhood would have been protected.

Those of us who grew up either in, or very near, the Adirondacks learn to edit ourselves when people ask where we live, and to say, "near Vermont" instead of "Northern New York" so as not to be confused with New York City or "upstate New York" which often refers to an area a mere hour north of New York City and considerably south of the Adirondacks. This is to say that "upstate New York," at least what people think of when they think "upstate," is south of "Northern New York." The Adirondack-y terrain continues north of the 'Blue Line' as well. When Viv of The Spy Who Loved Me, who grew up in eastern Canada, describes a childhood of fishing and hunting and swimming in fresh waters, she describes a childhood very much like my own.

The first birthday present I remember asking for was a fishing pole so I could go fishing with my grandfather in the Hudson River. The fish at this part of the river, the bend at Big Bay which was then considered West Glens Falls Pine trees are in abundance but is now part of Queensbury, are wholesome to eat, and I remember the pride of catching my very first sunfish and helping my mother to fry it in butter. When my parents first moved into the property they found the previous owners had left a strange rake, something like, but not quite a garden rake, and it turned out they had used this to gather the river mussels to eat. We never learned to use this, but the children enjoyed gathering river mussels by hand when swimming in the summer months.

We children would be excited when we found mussel shells, but they are brown and black, not the bright colors and varied shapes that ocean life can yield, so we didn't collect them. Our family didn't ice fish, as it was too dangerous to do so above swiftly moving water. However, the Adirondack lifestyle continued into the winter with cross-country skiing and hiking. Some nights it would get so cold that in bed I would be startled awake by a sharp crack like a gunshot. This was the sound of a tree cracking, something that sometimes happened, I was told, when the weather got below negative twenty Fahrenheit. When the cold broke in mid-March, ours was not the only family on the river to tap our maple trees and spend hours outside (had to be outside to avoid sticky walls) boiling the sap to syrup.

Brief History of the Adirondacks

The Adirondacks have been farmed, fished, lumbered, and used for recreation as long as there were people around the area. The earliest known claims to the Adirondacks were between the native Algonquins and Iroquois, but they did not live here. Old-timers say that the Native Americans viewed the mountains as haunted, but it seems to me the area was so inhospitable for habitation that it made more sense just to go into the mountains to hunt and fish, but then go home to where the winds didn't howl so fiercely and the temperature was not quite as brutal. The two groups had a rivalry over the waterways, now called Lake George and Lake Champlain, leading from what is now the southernmost tip of the Adirondacks to Canada, but they did not settle here.

The first non-native group to claim the Adirondacks were the Dutch, who called the area they controlled "New Netherland," which is both unimaginative and non-descriptive, as nothing in the rocky green wilderness resembled the temperate flat land of the Dutch. The Dutch also apparently believed the Adirondacks were a home for unicorns, so perhaps they didn't explore very well.

The next culture to claim control of the Adirondacks was the English, and that's when the deforestation really got going. The combination of timber and waterways from Quebec to the Hudson for transport was irresistible. Timber interests would buy land merely for the logs they could get from it, cut them down, and let the land go back to the state. It takes much less time to cut a tree down than for it to grow back, so they should have seen it would be a problem sooner than they did, but the trees in the Adirondacks seemed endless.

With the increase of tourism that resulted from W.H.H. Murray's book Adventures in the Wilderness, more planning was necessary to help people enjoy the Adirondacks while minimizing what is now called "environmental impact." As with any tourist venture, highlighting the beauties of the Adirondacks gave with one hand while taking away with the other. Any venture that makes an area more popular, by definition makes it less secret, less remote, less unknown, so the best thing Murray could have done for the Adirondacks might have been to shut up about them. The wealthy cognoscenti bought hundreds of acres of land and had laborers build "camps" on them which were really mansions only with a wild woods flavor. As counter-intuitive as it is, though, it was attention paid to the area by people building on it that led to environmental protections.

Sometimes trees would be cut down for even less than the wood. Hemlock trees were cut merely for the bark, used in tanning leather. Outside my window as I type this is a native Eastern Hemlock whose beauty has made me happy for the twenty odd years I have lived here and I am so glad that their destruction was slowed.

Generations of schoolchildren in and near the Adirondacks have been raised on the romance of loggers, brave, athletic, hardy, who cut the trees by hand, moved the logs with oxen, and floated them down the river to Glens Falls, where there is still a pulp mill. The practice of log drives continued until the 1950s (when trucks took over), and logging songs take their place next to sea shanties for romantic ballads. I was an adult when it occurred to me how horrific log drives must have been for the native fish and birds. I was also an adult when I realized that "brave" meant "this is a terribly dangerous job that would probably kill or maim you." When I saw those photos of men standing on moving logs, I used to just think of their bravery. Now, when I look at the photos of men standing on moving logs, I think about how I would never want someone I loved to take that job. You don't hear that much about the men that didn't make it. It should be noted that Crandall Public Library, the Central Reference Library of the Southern Adirondack Library System, was founded by a man considered to be one of the three best oxen drivers in the woods at the time. He made a fortune, and another man made a similar fortune, but the third was run over by a sled full of logs.

It was not, solely, the need to protect the trees that led to the creation of Adirondack Park. It was water that made it happen, the need for clean water, not in the Adirondacks, but in the bigger communities south, where the Hudson River flowed.

Vocal opposition to the exploitation of the Adirondacks became louder in the mid-1800s, with the writings of S.H. Hammond. His decrying of deforestation spurred Verplanck Colvin to call for a protected area, and Adirondack Forest Preserve was created in 1885. This protected forests but did not demand the destruction of buildings and roads already in the area. A few years later, in 1892, the Adirondack Park was created, and the map which showed the protected areas had the outline written in blue, hence the term 'the Blue Line.' Native Adirondackers still refer to themselves as "living inside the Blue Line." The State of New York was not, and is not, the only entity protecting the Adirondacks. The Adirondack Mountain Club, founded in 1922, exists not only for the big picture of park protection but for the more practical day to day purpose of maintaining hiking trails and providing lodging for hikers. Those who have never been on a herd path may not understand the importance of maintained trails, but they are an essential part of protecting the wilderness, as necessary as paved roads are for drivers. The Adirondack Park is unique; land can be owned by individuals within its borders. Not everyone is, or was, enamored of the protections. "Playground for the rich," my normally sweet-natured mother used to hiss. She and my father had moved to Glens Falls from Saranac Lake, and often I would hear of businesses that had been proposed for the area only to be prevented by environmental protections. I didn't understand the "playground for the rich" complaint, as hiking was a relatively inexpensive pastime, but this was before I understood that environmental protections made it so hard to earn a living in the woods that people whose families had lived there for generations were being forced off properties by rising taxes they could never hope to earn the money to pay.

"Playground for the rich" didn't even begin to describe the exclusivity of certain Adirondack treasures. Sure, you could hike anywhere. But what if you wanted to enjoy the view from the Lake Placid Club? You'd better have a membership, and money alone was not enough to get you in. The Lake Placid Club, founded in 1895, prohibited its use from Jews and Blacks for most of its existence, with the tantalizingly exclusive phrase "regardless of merit." If Disraeli had shown up on Queen Victoria's arm he would have been turned away. (Well, he died in

1871, but the point stands.) Adirondack Park is vast, as Fleming has his heroine observe in the first few pages of The Spy Who Loved Me. The acres of private and public land that comprise the park are more than all four major national parks combined, as big, in fact, as the size of our neighboring state of Vermont. As a "park" it is a puzzle, though, as privately-owned houses and businesses are well inside the 'Blue Line.' The 'Blue Line' refers to the early designation of where the protected land would be.

Protected land in the Adirondack Park has different designations. Wilderness is the most protected; in Wilderness areas there is no building, no paving of roads, and no motorized vehicles are allowed on public trails. Wild Forest areas may allow motorized vehicles, but no new construction and no paved roads.

The protections of the Adirondack Park, however, didn't tear down existing buildings or level towns, they just made rules for use of property. For this reason, you can be in the Adirondack Park, on a sidewalk having your bagel breakfast, before heading onto a trail where you won't see another person for days.

In The Spy Who Loved Me, Ian Fleming does a good job of explaining the push and pull between environmental concerns and tourism, and between the haves and the have nots. The book takes place in 1961, and here's how he describes October.

"Apparently October fifteenth is a kind of magical date in this particular holiday world. Everything closes down on that day, except along the major highways. It is supposed to be the beginning of winter. There is the hunting season coming up, but the rich hunters have their own hunting clubs and camps in the mountains, and the poor ones take their cars to one or another of the picnic areas and climb up into the forests before dawn to get their deer. Anyway, around October fifteenth the tourists disappear from the scene and there is no more easy money to be made in the Adirondacks." The tourist season was slightly shorter in the 1960s, before we consciously made tourism out of our beautiful autumn leaves. As a native Northern New Yorker, I have often been met with surprise from people from more temperate climates, that we leave perfectly good buildings, empty half the year. We get used to this.

I set out, in the glory of an Adirondack August, to explore every tourist site that was still in existence and would have been available to my 1960s heroine, and also to visit the locations of those no longer in business. After I got to the Canadian border, I turned right around and went to my prearranged cabin to go to bed early. I had a big day of sightseeing ahead of me. The joys were many.

Chapter 3

Sights That Ian Probably Missed
What impressed me in the Adirondacks, From the North to the South

Ausable Chasm

I would say the most magnificent sight of the entire trip. was Ausable Chasm. I don't even know where to begin, so I will start with my childhood memories. There was not a time I didn't remember seeing bumper stickers, t-shirts, and flyers for Ausable Chasm, and from my first being able to read my question was the same as many who ask me about it today: How do you pronounce that?

"Ka zm." It is pronounced Aw-say-bull Kasm. Chasm isn't exactly a word used in everyday conversation, so even knowing how to say it I still wasn't sure what it was. If you look up the word in the dictionary, it will say "deep fissure in a rock." If you look at the publicity materials, they will say Ausable Chasm is "the Grand Canyon of the East." It seemed to me as a child, and still does seem, that if it were as magnificent as the Grand Canyon we would know more about it, so I will say that Ausable Chasm is something very much in between a "fissure" and the Grand Canyon. Ausable, by the way, means "of the sand" and the rock is "Potsdam sandstone," referring to a small town just north of Adirondack Park. Ausable Chasm has been run as a tourist attraction since 1870, and if you call them for information, the recording begins by telling you that this is the oldest attraction in the country.

The area is beautiful. The Ausable River has relentlessly twisted its way down and through the rock in such a way as to make it possible to take boats down the river, during which you have views of rock faces over a hundred feet high. One hundred feet is, in its own way, magnificent, yet I would venture to say this is somewhat less than the Grand Canyon.

If you are driving on Route 9 through the area, you'll see signs saying Ausable Chasm, and you can pause and take pictures, and you may think that the bridge from the road is sufficient. It is not. The view from the bridge, while breathtaking, is as one chocolate chip from the most luscious cookie you have ever tasted. Admission to the chasm is about as much as a really nice meal out, but the price is worth it, would be so even if just to see the tremendous feats of engineering necessary to make it safe to be there. The line for admission, which was in the main building, was long, but this was partially, because people were trying to keep six feet apart from

The Ausable River from above

one another. Everyone was masked, but I knew I would feel safer when we were outside again. When I was already in the line, I was told it would be over an hour from entering the line to the desk, and I was already committed before I knew that. I was also already in line when I found out that the shortest tour was about three hours, which was a The Ausable River from above problem because I needed to go to the bathroom. Luckily, there was a bathroom before getting on the boats.

From the admission area, everyone got a wrist band designating the type of tour. Boat? Hiking only? Rappelling? I love to rappel but chose a boat tour because rappelling would not have been available during the 1960s to my heroine.

The first few steps on the tour of Ausable Chasm are not promising. There's a sidewalk, a fence, and a lot of twisted metal on display during your walk from the front gate (past the bathroom!) to the chasm proper. Historical markers tell of the tourist history of the chasm, and how a terrible flood one year ruined the method of viewing the chasm.

This had involved huge wooden boats, seating sixty, and guiding. One of the former guide boats rails drilled into the rock. At a cost of millions, the rails were rebuilt after the flood and they proudly resumed business, only to have everything swept away again. At this point they switched from twenty-foot boats

One of the former guideboats

On the boat tour at Ausable Chasm

to rubber rafts that seat about ten, which are more maneuverable, and which require no guiding rails. I walked past the markers, crossed the street, and then through a beautiful woods. The river, on my left, was obscured just a bit by the gorgeous August greenery, and the air, so oppressively hot in the parking lot, became sweet and pleasant in the woods. In places the trail went seemingly dangerously close to the cliff, and I marveled

at how in the world previous chasm workers had made paths and guard rails that stayed fastened to the rock. Rock doves (that's the proper name for pigeons) had several homes on the cliffs, and the air buzzed with summer insects, so I was glad I had packed lots of insect repellent.

First the walk was through the woods, then it was down. Down down, down, down stone stairs, down a narrow, piny path, until there was an incongruous boat dock. It seemed so out of place in the ancient, mostly unadorned rock. Two stations were at that rock, the first to get a life jacket, and the next to get in the boat.

Because I am short, I always try to be in the front of the boat, the train, the movie theater, wherever I am, but in this case I was glad to let the person get ahead of me; a man with his two preschool=aged children. He and the kids got in, I was in the row behind with a man who seemed nice, and the boat filled in with people and a few extra paddles.

Floating on the water was a different and wonderful feeling from the scooter. At the end of the trip we took a bus back to the parking lot. The man who had been next to me in the boat said, "This trip was so worth it, but the parking was terrible!"

"I didn't have any trouble finding a spot. I'm on a scooter." "That was you? That's a sweet little machine!" I was tickled.

Before leaving the chasm, in the parking lot, I opened up the seat of my scooter and got my packed food for a snack: plums from the Farmers' Market at home, cherry tomatoes from my garden, and a granola bar. The plums were a little worse for wear from all the road vibrations, but still tasty and sweet, and I had thought ahead to pack tomatoes that were slightly orange, so they were very good, not at all crushed from the ride.

Underground Railroad Museum

After my snack, I went on to another not-to-be missed attraction of this area, the North Star Underground Railroad Museum. When I say "in this area" I mean that the Underground Railroad Museum is so close to the main building of Ausable Chasm that it was unclear to me at first whether they were part of the same organization.

Founded in 2011 and located in a solidly built and beautifully-detailed house, you'd think from the outside that the museum might be well-meaning but slapdash, just artifacts in a historic building. This was my worry because although I enjoy small museums, my experience with house museums has been uneven, and I had not heard much about this one before happening to come across it. This is a museum of high standards and excellent volunteer and professional staff.

The North Star Underground Railroad Museum

The front desk had free masks of good quality fabric. I "bought" one to cover my entrance, which was by suggested donation. Right away, though, I knew this was no hack job, since as people came in they were asked to wait for a docent. The docent didn't guide us all through the house but gave an overview of how the museum could be best enjoyed and understood before recommending the path we took and leaving us to do this at our own pace.

They named names, and it was a shock to learn that the Platt family, for whom Plattsburgh was named and which I never gave any thought to, not only

The quaint cabins of the Shamrock Inn

participated The North Star Underground Railroad Museum in slavery but actively campaigned for it. That seems to be rather an important family trait and I was shocked that I had never heard this before. Maybe I had, I wondered, and just wasn't paying attention. When I looked the Platt family up online it turned out that biographers didn't consider this important, not in the Wikipedia entry nor in several others I found.

You won't want to miss the brilliant story of John Thomas, who escaped slavery in Maryland and founded a farm here in Northern New York. You should not miss, but may not be able to endure, the heartbreaking historical video. Because the museum is mostly self-guided, you can decide for yourself what is most important to you, but by all means do not miss The North Star Underground Railroad Museum.

Shamrock Inn

The quaint cabins of the Shamrock Inn

I had come to my day at Ausable Chasm from a night at a tiny motel, the kind that's all little cabins, in Peru, New York. It occurs to me as I write this that I have lived in Northern New York all my life but had never set foot in one of these before. Then again, why would I? I live here, and usually don't need to vacation here.

You would perhaps think that cabin hotels only appeared after highways were ubiquitous, but many are one hundred years old, and while not many are still in operation, those that are tend to

A welcome sight, the Shamrock Inn sign

be family owned. Those no longer in operation were built so sturdily that their relics can be seen on Route 9 here and there from at least Malta, New York to just before the Canadian border. Sturdy, yes, but not built for winter; each domicile being a separate bit of housing makes me shudder at the thought of heating them in the winter, and I don't know of such a motel that is open for more than the summer season. They look tiny from the outside, but the one I was in was more spacious than most hotel rooms and most studio apartments where I A welcome sight, the Shamrock Inn sign have stayed.

I stayed at a place called The Shamrock Inn, owned by an energetic, blythe, youthful woman named Anne Marie. I found her and her marvelous motel on my reconnaissance trip the week before my real trip. I put some rules on myself before re-creating the 1960s trip, and one of these was to stay, as much as possible, in places that would have been in existence when my fictional heroine was traveling. Such places often don't have web pages, even in 2021, so I figured the best way to find a motel on Route 9 was to stop at every appealing motel on Route 9 during my recon and to ask if they had room the following week.

The Shamrock Inn, like "Dreamy Pines" in the book I was copying, has cabins approximately in a half circle, facing the road. It's not quite as well appointed as Dreamy Pines, lacking a swimming pool, a lake, and a restaurant. The main building, however, has a cozy little patio with self serve coffee if you happen to get up before the host. This patio also has a magnificent grill guests can use, which seems to me alarmingly trusting on the part of the owner. What was most impressive to me about The Shamrock Inn, after my delight at its being from the right time period, is its perfect, pragmatic beauty.

There's a book called What Not to Build which showcases how designers and builders, even with ample money and planning time, can mess up a design from installing the wrong size window, or selecting window shades out of balance with the room, or making a winding path when a straight one would have looked better. Most of us have been in a house or seen a painting where there was just something "off" in the design, something that makes us anxious in the way it came out. We've also been in chairs that were terribly expensive but uncomfortable, or walked directly from the outside into someone's foyer where they decided to go right for the white floor instead of putting in a mud room or even just a dark entry carpet. Such mistakes make people feel uncomfortable, or unwelcome. There was nothing of that sort at the Shamrock Inn. Everything Anne Marie touched, painted, decorated, or purchased to put in a room, is a perfect balance in terms of color, design, and utility. The chairs in the little patio outside the main building are sturdy and well padded, but not so padded that you sink into them. The grill is at an attractive angle that makes it possible to easily turn your head and talk to the people you are grilling for. Outside the patio is a garden of mixed food plants and

The Ausable Marsh at sunrise

flowers, pretty and practical without giving you the idea that you are intruding on Anne Marie's real source of food by walking through them to the patio. The signage on the patio telling guests to help themselves is friendly and clear.

Each cabin has a comfortable and period appropriate chair on the porch, and a simple, attractive sign with the cabin number. Inside, the linens are a light and breezy color, the walls white, but not a too bright white, the art simple and in a perfect size and arrangement for a small space. I had to ask, "Are you an artist?" She cheerfully said her only outlet for art was decorating cabins.

Ausable Marsh

It was exciting to get up after a night at the Shamrock Inn. I could relax, because I had done the difficult part - I had gotten to Canada! --and begun to enjoy the sites on the way back. I had been longing to see Ausable Marsh, and was eager to do so at sunrise, when I'd be most likely to see the more timid animals and birds. I was not disappointed. Ausable Marsh is a wetland part of Lake Champlain, southeast. It has been protected since 1950 and has walking paths, bike trails, and a campground. As you go from Route 9, down the path to the marsh itself, elaborate full color signs identify plants and animals. They are a bit faded, but readable.

A beautiful spot

I found a sandy part of beach and was surprised at that. In my section of the state, we have only rocks, not sand, near our lakes. We have so much rock in the Lake George area that the village of Lake George had to buy sand from New Jersey for its beach. And the truth is, as I discovered when I took off my shoes, that the sand of Lake Champlain is different from the sand of The Garden State, feeling different between the toes, which I attributed to Lake Champlain sand and to fresh water having fewer varieties of shells. It is particles of shells, not rock, that make up much of an ocean beach.

That morning, the sun came up a golden orange. I sat on a fallen log and watched the beautiful herons wading. When I tried to get closer, to get a picture, they took off, moving their immense wings with a slow majesty that seems ineffective for flight. Not ineffective. Just marvelous.

I saw a beaver house and listened to the morning call of bullfrogs as long as I could, then headed back to my cabin to pack. It was a lovely morning.

Sculpture Garden

Very near the town of Peru and the Shamrock Inn is a sculpture garden. This represents one artist, working in found objects of mostly iron, and the sculptures are over eight feet tall and perhaps four feet wide. These magnificent, non-objective pieces are arranged whimsically in a mowed field, I expect in the hope that passers by will purchase them. There is no expectation of payment to look, just an appealing little sign in-book by the entrance that also lists prices. The costs were out of my price range, but I signed the book and took a business card. You never know.

Keeseville

Headed south, the next village was Keeseville. Keeseville, New York, is a town I still don't know well, because mostly what I did there was visit the library. But I was

Stoneledge Sculpture Garden

grateful for this library! Since everyone is expected to have a cell phone these days, pay phones are difficult to find, so, in the world's weird circular logic, it was imperative I carry and charge a cell phone. This is true even though there are many places in the Adirondacks that cell phones do not work, cell phone desserts, they call them, where no tower has been set up and no city exists to link your phone to others. I used the phone whenever I did have a connection, making videos both for future reference and to send to my sponsors to thank them for making the trip possible. For this reason, my phone lost power quickly. Thank goodness for libraries, which, as a rule, have free Wi-Fi.

The Keeseville library is a small brick structure built for its own function. This is interesting, as in small towns, often the library was previously a house or office building. Also, in small towns the library tends to have limited hours, so I was lucky the day I was there to find it open. The librarian (and I mean librarian, a trained person with a Master's Degree in Information Science) was friendly and knowledgeable and had built an impressive small collection. The librarian also welcomed local artists, and a beautiful pottery show was on display. The craftsmanship was excellent and the prices reasonable, and it made me ache that I could not buy anything. I simply could not fit so much as an extra mug in my milk crate.

The main room as you go in is mostly adult fiction. Because I used to be a Children's Librarian, I asked where the Children's Room was. As is typical for a small library, this collection is in the basement, with the lights off if no one was there. But the librarian showed me the light switch and let me have free rein.

The Children's Collection in the Keeseville Free Library is, I am happy to say, up to date, clean, relevant, and, for the size of the library, very large. The furniture is sturdy, brightly colored, and easy to keep clean. And-hooray--I easily found a place to charge my phone. I read a children's book while I waited for my phone to get above fifty percent, and at that point I checked my messages. There was nothing that could not wait.

After hours of sunshine on the scooter, it was a blessing to be able to enjoy the cool quiet of the Keeseville Library, right there on Route 9. Actually, I stopped at the Keeseville library more than once, once when it was open, and once, when it was closed, but I used the free Wi-Fi on the back steps, overlooking a grand stretch of the Ausable River.

The river there is deep and so fast that if I could have gotten to the water there, I would not have gone in. But in the park, overlooking it, it was beautiful, with a rumble that was less than a roar and beautiful rapids there were just less than a waterfall.

After I rested for a while, I got a slice of pizza at a shop, Giuseppe's, a nice place near the library. It was cool and dark in the restaurant, and the pizza had the most delectable spinach, just the right amount, fresh spinach, not canned.

Keeseville seems to have an air of political awareness. Most shop windows had flyers advertising not only upcoming events, but asking for involvement, such as "Save our Historic Bridges." Keeseville is small but endearing. I would like to spend more time there.

Trail Heads

All down Route 9, on both the east and west sides of the road, are signs designating trail heads. "Trail head" seems an odd term to me. In Adirondack terms, it means the beginning of an official, groomed and designated trail. My family used to call the trails in the Adirondacks "follow the dot" trails, referring to the round, palm-sized markers affixed to trees which tell us,

Prospect Mt. Trail

Poke-O-Moonshine Mountain

based on their color, which route we are on. I love follow the dot trails, which make me feel like I am a real hiker on a discovery at the same time as they keep me from becoming lost.

There are many mountains you can visit from Route 9 trailheads, and some take days to summit while others are merely a nice day hike. There's even one you can drive up. In the book, our heroine says, "There was hardly an old fort, museum, waterfall, cave or high mountain I didn't visit" but I doubt this, at least about the mountains. The weather is so changeable in the Adirondacks, the locations so remote, and hiking such a strenuous activity that even a day hike takes planning and equipment, things that Viv does not mention.

Prospect Mt. Trail

She might, of course, have hiked up Prospect Mountain. That is probably the shortest hike on Route 9. But it is relentless, no switchbacks, as it follows an old cog railway that naturally had to go straight up, and with Viv's/Fleming's flair for detail it seems there would have been a description, a triumphant paragraph when she reached the top. (There is no question of Fleming himself climbing Prospect, as he was writing this book he was already very ill from what would eventually kill him, the combined effects of an early heart attack and continued smoking and Poke-O-Moonshine Mountain drinking.) Viv might have driven her little Vespa up Prospect, except the highway had not been constructed yet, so she would have had to walk. Even if the highway had been built in 1961, the story takes place in October, long after the Highway has closed for the year. No indeed, either Viv the character was lying (and she is meant to be a reliable narrator) or Fleming just put in the bit about climbing mountains to make the reader respect her more.

It is a shame that Fleming was too ill to climb when he was researching places for Viv to experience. There's nothing like hiking in the Adirondacks. From the very first step onto a trail, I am exhilarated. I love signing my name in the register, hoping to see friends' names, and I sometimes do. I love the scent of the woods, fresh and clean in the spring, even with the mud, and comfortingly earthy in the fall. I love feeling the season change as I gain altitude. Is it late spring? Climb a few hundred feet and you'll see the plants of a few weeks ago, climb down again and your calendar adjusts itself. Is it early autumn? Gain an hour's worth of altitude and it is late autumn or even winter.

I enjoy the precariousness of climbing, the care it takes, paradoxically, to make a day carefree: A day hike where you remember to pack enough snacks and layers and a good map will likely be delightful, but forget one layer of wool, or neglect to pack a hat, and the cold of the bare summit will send you scrambling to the safety and warmth of a lower elevation, even on a warm spring day.

During COVID lockdown and during the times of greatest precaution, I was able to hike more than I had in years. Unless I started very early in the morning, the trail would get busy, even on non-High Peaks, but I was grateful for the safe outside activity, and for the fact that, other things being canceled, my teen daughter who had never much been interested in hiking learned to love it. Well, not to love it enough to make it a habit after COVID restrictions were somewhat lifted, but to enjoy it enough to go with me sometimes and to listen to me prattle on about the beautiful trees, rocks, and animals.

I didn't pack enough food or enough layers for a day hike on my trek, but I gazed with fondness at the trail heads for Poke-O-Moonshine, Prospect, and the like. I'll go back soon, but if I intend to go hiking, I probably will not go on a scooter.

The Adirondack History Museum in Elizabethtown

Adirondack History Museum

The next town headed south on Route 9, in fact, halfway home but solidly in the Adirondacks, was Elizabethtown. In the old High School building in Elizabethtown is a museum called the Adirondack History Museum, which is pretty ambitious for such a small space. After all, the Adirondacks are about the same size as the entire state of Vermont, and we are going to

The Adirondack History Museum in Elizabethtown expect to get all the history from an old High School?

I have been, many times, to the Adirondack Experience (formerly Adirondack Museum)

Modern art in the Adirondacks

at Blue Mountain Lake, and was a little sorry for the Adirondack History Museum, going in. I didn't need to be. Adirondack History Museum has its own niche, its own charm. I would call it "metal" in staking out its own claim to the narrative.

The building is so old that the side entrances bear signs for "Boys" and "Girls." The old main entrance is unmistakable, but now that it is a museum, not a school, you go in an unprepossessing side door near a small parking lot and a huge new piece of modern art.

I mean it when I say "huge," I mean you are meant to climb on it. This piece is a grey wooden globe, with two sets of almost spiral stairs going

The fire tower at the Adirondack History Museum

Modern art in the Adirondacks to the top, so of course I did, to get a look at the world around me. It was nice.

I was told by the staff inside the building that the artist had just finished painting this impressive thing a few hours before I arrived, and indeed, there was paint on individual blades of grass next to the thing. I felt lucky to be there when I was.

Speaking of climbing, the Adirondack History Museum boasts a fire tower, yes indeed, a real, formerly in use, fire tower and they let you climb it. Not only do they let you climb it, you get a head start; you start the climb about a third of the way up by going from an inside exhibit, through a side door, to a tower platform. The day I was there was sunny and warm, but windy. As I climbed, I read the signs that identified the trees I was climbing past and was happy to see a native hemlock just like the one in my own backyard.

As you climb higher in any fire tower, even on a still day, it feels more and more rickety, and on a windy day I had to remind myself how very many people had made it safely to the top and down again, before I did.

Even with the wind, it was a thrill to be in the fire tower, and I got a chuckle about the experience of being there without first having to climb a mountain. The view, of a village rather than acres and acres of trees, was still picture postcard beautiful.

I love fire towers and climb every mountain (that is reasonable to conquer) that has one, but have wondered for years what good they do. Okay, say you know the mountain is on fire. THEN what? Bring buckets up the mountain?

It seemed that the remoteness of the Adirondacks would make fighting fires a challenge, and I will tell a story to illustrate this. Once I was on my roller blades, on the bike trail between Glens Falls and Lake George, and the bank was on fire. I suppose someone walking or biking must have dropped a cigarette. It was August, and dry and breezy, and I looked around for a stream–not that I knew what to do with a stream if I saw one. On your bike or blades you don't bring more than a small water bottle, which is too small to use against a fire. Anyway, that part of the trail had no stream, so, feeling both desperate and ridiculous, I sped off on my blades to the nearest road and the nearest business. And yes, it took some time for the business owner to understand the problem and to call 911, but the fire department got the fire out.

This story took place on flat ground. With telephones. What did they do in the mountains in 1935?

I posted this question on the History and Legends of the Adirondacks Facebook page and received wonderful answers. From the fire tower, the ranger would shoot an azimuth to determine the exact location, radio the nearest village, and fire experts would be dispatched with yes, buckets of water, but also axes and shovels–shovels to dig ditches to stop fires in their paths. If there were not enough fire fighters around, high school students would be excused from classes to fight fires, and I can't decide whether this is cool or insanity.

We get to climb fire towers in museums now because they are not needed so much on the mountains, both because of modern communications and because of better managed mountains. It's worth noting that in The Spy Who Loved Me, the main character is terrified and saddened when it looks as though the bad guys are going to burn the hotel, because she is sure this will lead to an Adirondack conflagration.

Adirondack History Museum is one fine museum, worthy of the name. It has art, outdoors, social history, modern social commentary, an heirloom garden, and an impressive gift shop with Arto Monaco mementos. Arto Monaco is fondly remembered by locals as the brain and the brawn behind The Land of Make Believe, a theme park for small children, and Storytown, U.S.A., on Route 9 in Queensbury, New York, but more on that later.

A piece of Arto Monaco's work at the museum

It turns out that the layout of a school is exactly suited to a museum whose displays are so distinct and so compartmentalized. I hardly knew where to start. With entire rooms devoted to such subjects as the history of Woman Suffrage, the Forty Six highest peaks, Social History, and the artist Arto Monaco, the museum was just the right size for a morning's visit. The hallway space was used to display socially conscious art, and the fire tower was outside the door of the High Peaks room.

A whole room dedicated to Arto Monaco is, to me, the least of what this great man deserves. I knew and loved Arto, loved him as one loves a beloved great uncle that you don't get too emotionally close to but wish you could. I worked with him one summer at Storytown, U.S.A. when it had so recently made the change to Six Flags - The Great Escape that the stationery was still in the supply closet. He was one of three staff artists, Arto, along with John Kennison, and Robert Vorreyer (called Bob). They were all nice, though. Arto specialized at the time in woodwork, rejuvenating old carousel horses. John did most of the signs. Bob was also a celebrated artist, although I did not get as close to him as to Arto. All three artists welcomed me to eat my lunches with them in the shop, and I remember wanting to touch the beautiful carousel horses, but never daring to. A particular animal that Arto was working on, he told me, was worth thirty thousand dollars even before he was done.

One such animal was in the lobby of The Great Escape, so called after Six Flags Amusement Parks bought Storytown, U.S.A., was a tiger, rather than a horse. One day an elegant elderly woman came in, gave her name, and said she was there to meet Mr. Wood for lunch. I buzzed Mr. Wood and, for some reason, while she was waiting, this elegant woman decided to jump on the back of the priceless tiger. "Ma'am, you can't do that," I said. Predictably, the woman asserted her right to be on the tiger with a "Do you know who I am?" I said, "I know you are Mrs. Whitney, but Mr. Wood signs my paychecks and he doesn't want anybody on those carousel animals." Marylou Whitney, (birth name Schroeder, name at death Hendrickson) was an American socialite, and the doyenne of the Saratoga racing scene, known for her fabulous parties celebrating the racing season over which she reigned for years.

What conversations went on later between Marylou Whitney and Charles R. Wood, I don't know, but she got off Arto's carousel tiger and I never heard anything more about it.

Years later, Mrs. Whitney stopped giving her annual gala in Saratoga Springs and gave her money to the backstretch workers, creating an organization that provided those who care for the horses with health care, translation services, education, and entertainment. Being a backstretch worker is a killer job and I respected her for making that change.

I don't remember whether I told Arto about the tiger. I probably didn't, because it embarrassed me, and anyway, at the time I was in school to be an Art Historian and I wouldn't have wanted Arto to hear me complain. Arto's career was long and varied, from his WWII art to his last days working for Mr. Charley Wood. One of my first areas of awareness of an art style came to me when I noticed, as a pre-teen, that the people painted at the Great Escape looked very much like the ones in Magic Forest, another Lake George fun park. If I had thought about it at the time, I would have believed that Arto's entire career was illustrating theme parks.

Now that I am in my fifties, it is of great interest to me that Arto's theme park illustrations were his twilight job. I wouldn't call it "retirement job," because he worked too hard for me to think of this as retirement. Arto's heartfelt project was, of course, The Land of Make Believe, a park designed for young children, right down to everything being child-sized. Swept away by the flooding of the Ausable River in 1979, some of the small structures have a home in what is now The Great Escape.

The Arto Monaco room at the Adirondack History Museum is efficiently designed, using all the space reasonably possible with a frieze of Arto work running along the wall, and his history on sub walls in the room. It is a lot to take in.

There's a color scheme, a brightness that is more than pastel, but less than offensively vivid, that is particular to Arto work, and is easily seen when several pieces are next to one another. But that's for the illustrations for children. Arto's other work included cartooning, interior design, making training aids–he seemed to be able to apply his artistic talent to anything he touched, even his work in the army.

The "Community Ties" exhibit is rather a catch all. It contains desks, an old piano and stories of school days of yore, but also an account of a murder, with the mementos in a case in the back of the room. The school benches are things of beauty that I didn't realize were beauty when I was forced to sit at them in my own school years and thought how old fashioned they were.

I was terribly uncomfortable in the exhibit "Hiking in the Adirondack High Peaks." The "Forty-Six" refers to the peaks believed at one time to have summits above four thousand feet, that is, the tallest mountains in the Adirondacks. Some have maintained trails, some have herd paths, some you need to be good with a compass to summit. If you have never climbed in the Adirondacks but have, for example, climbed in the White Mountains, you might find climbing Adirondack Mountains a particular challenge, because the climb is generally not directly up.

Our mountains, which are, technically, eroded plains, roll, and the paths twist both to get around rock faces and to reach summits of mountains that have multiple little hills in the way. So, climbing in the Adirondacks is more than exercise; it can be a heady, I-did-it! experience, even for the smaller mountains. To put it bluntly, forty-sixing as an activity needs to stop. We need to stop encouraging this damaging, arrogant practice of climbing the highest and most environmentally vulnerable peaks. Here's the thing: the room is nicely arranged, and by "nicely" I mean attractively, invitingly. Every artifact, every display in this room is designed to make you think climbing the highest peaks is to be lauded.

It was a great accomplishment at one time, to climb all those mountains, but now it is so easily done that a nearby summer camp has a program wherein the campers do all the forty-six in five weeks. In the corner of the 46-room is a screen on which a video of Grace Hudowalski plays. Grace was the first woman to climb all forty-six peaks, started the club that became the Adirondack 46-ers, and even in her later years answered every petition to be in the club. In the video that plays in the museum, this elegant and articulate woman describes her climbs in the old days.

My first job out of college, I worked for the Adirondack Mountain Club. I loved it. I was working to protect the environment, learning a great deal about hiking and camping and running a not-for-profit. It was while working for the Adirondack Mountain Club that I learned about the importance of maintaining real trails as opposed to herd paths, and about the dangers of everybody going on the same trails. I also learned that the term "forever wild" has to be employed with some flexibility. The woods can't both be "forever wild" and have maintained trails, but the benefits in terms of lack of erosion and lesser likelihood of fire make trail maintenance a paradoxically necessary part of wilderness.

Inez Milholland on her white horse

Back then, it was expected, as an employee, that I would spend as much of my free time as I could hiking or canoeing, which suited me fine. I had never in my life been interested in climbing the forty-six, and it was an eye opener when I attempted to do so. The other staff at Adirondack Mountain Club had warned me what I would see, but I was not prepared for it. I was not prepared for the deterioration of highly popular trails caused by human interaction.

So many feet had stepped on the trail to Cascade that the way route had become, at least for the first half mile, a great big U, as if a bulldozer had bulldozed a route for a subway. That huge trench was the result of mud being picked up on feet, and feet trampling the trail. And for what? The view on Cascade was magnificent, but not more impressive than many views from smaller but less traveled mountains. The deterioration that results from more feet on already popular trails is completely optional. We can make a choice not to make it worse. And surely the accomplishment of being a 46-er 15,000 must be weighed against the horrible environmental impact gaining that now less-impressive patch means.

Okay, I confess: I finished Cascade and Porter on the same day, and I sent my paper letter to Grace Hudowalski asking for her to record my trip, and I received a lovely personalized letter in return. I knew I'd never climb another 46, but I had the letter to treasure from that great lady, whose accomplishments were indeed extraordinary.

It makes me very sad to see that in the room about the forty-six (which aren't even really all forty-six of them, above four thousand feet) there is not a sign saying: please don't do this. Please climb less traveled mountains. That's my advice. There is such a sign on Route 9, by the way, but you have to already be on Route 9 to see it, by a trail head.

The Adirondack Suffragists exhibit was amazing, particularly the focus on Inez Milholland. I feel as though I had never heard of Inez Milholland before this summer, and then she was everywhere. There is a plaque honoring her on Route 9, in Lewis, New York, where she is buried. I read that trying to make myself remember why I should know her. She was prominently featured at the Adirondack History Museum. And, as luck would have it, she was a character in a Suffrage Pageant that was organized by a staff member at the library where I work, and I was asked to be in this pageant. I didn't play Inez, but as Alice Paul I passed the torch of liberty to the actor who portrayed her.

Inez is not as well-known as Susan B. Anthony or Elizabeth Cady Stanton, which, now that I know her story, puzzles me. Inez was a dynamo. She was a labor lawyer, an athlete, a war correspondent, believed in free love, and died a romantic and tragic death (1916), leaving her work to her grieving sister. She was beautiful and brave, even leading a suffrage procession on horseback. Why doesn't this woman have a movie? The more I learn about Inez, the more I love her, and you can learn so much by going to the Adirondack History Museum, where she takes her place, not just with, but ahead of the better known feminists of her day.

The last exhibit I enjoyed at the Adirondack History Museum was "Transportation" - sledges and bikes and carriages, beautifully arranged in the cool ground floor of the museum. By this time my brain was full, and I was eager to get back on the road, myself.

In the gift shop is a case full of mementos from Arto's Land of Make Believe. These are still in their original boxes, with the prices from the old days marked next to today's prices. I bought a charm to give to one of my employees, an artist herself with a love for Arto.

Elizabethtown

Pulling the scooter into the parking lot of the Halfway House motel, I began to wonder, for the first time, if maybe this was a stupid idea. There wasn't a hotel or campground anywhere on Route 9 from the Canadian border to Glens Falls with a vacancy on a Saturday night, and the owner of this place had graciously offered to let me camp "behind the hotel, next to the river." That was a lovely thought and a generous offer, so why was I nervous?

Well, I'd never met these people before the conversation the week before that led to this moment. I didn't know them. Maybe they'd try to kill me in my sleep. I was comforted by the fact that I had nothing of value to kill for, nothing but a borrowed scooter--and the owner's wife already owned one. No, it wasn't my hosts. The nerves came from not having camped in years, and in having to face that fear.

Oh, I'd camped, and a lot, before my now teenaged daughter was born. I'd primitive-camped in the High Peaks, and I even spent an odd period of my life proud to be a primitive winter camper. I had fond memories of hiking in Sorrels, with a pack that was a quarter to a third my own weight, eager to eat all the chocolate and fat I craved, because you can do that when you are winter camping. Sleeping in a lean-to in a sleeping bag rated to negative thirty Fahrenheit made me proud, hot chocolate on a single burner camp stove delighted me. These were risky behaviors, requiring real planning and skill, and I had mastered them, so why was I worried about mere tenting by the Boquet River? I didn't even have to carry a pack anywhere. I drove the scooter to the riverbank.

I guess there were too many "what ifs," and I'd hiked enough to know the risks, but not recently enough to be confident I'd anticipated everything sufficiently. What if it rained on my little tent? Well, I'd packed a rain fly, in effect, a plastic tablecloth, but I'd had no chance to test whether it would stand up to real rain or stay put if it was windy. What if I didn't fit in the five feet of space it gave me? I would have to endure being cramped for one night, I told myself, and surely it could be no worse than airplane seats where I'd often slept calmly overnight. What if,

The busy bees.

on this moonless night, I had to go to the bathroom, tripped, and fell into the river? Okay, that one I had to just hope didn't happen.

When the owner said "behind the hotel," I had thought he meant a few feet. But he directed me to a winding path someone had cleared, wide enough for a car and packed down enough that I was confident the scooter wouldn't fall over, that went for about a quarter mile before it came to the Boquet. (Boquet, when referring to the river, is correctly spelled without the u in the first syllable and pronounced bo-ket, even though, I have heard, it is indeed named after a gathering of flowers.)

The bank of the river is flat here, with ample places to set up a tent, and lots of untended mounds of grass. I had not had room to pack a sleeping mat, but the grass was not the packed to the near-concrete firmness of a real campground and I breathed a sigh of relief realizing the grass would be soft enough to rest upon. Because there were clouds, I parked the scooter under a tree, and pitched the tent nearby, facing the river. I was tickled that the only tent I could fit in the milk crate, a child's play tent, was covered in vivid pictures of dinosaurs and unicorns.

As soon as the tent was up, I was in the river. I had put my clothes over my bathing suit when dressing that morning because I didn't know whether there would be a place to change when I got to the Boquet. I simply pulled off my t-shirt and leggings and went into the swirling river.

Well, not quite. There was a mini cliff of dirt, about eight feet, no real path to the water. I lowered myself on my arms most of the way and dropped down to the sand, then walked on rounded pebbles to the edge of the river. The Boquet here is a good fly-fishing river, which, if you know fly fishing, means it is not very deep. However, there are abundant pools where the water is over a short person's head, and it was very hot, so I was eager to submerge myself.

First, though, since I'd never been in this river, I checked for leeches and snapping turtles, walking slowly in the wonderful cool water, letting my feet submerge, looking, looking. I saw no leeches. Good. No turtles. Also good. A few footprints that seemed to be deer on the bank. Oooh, maybe I would see one in the early morning, I thought, then went deeper in the water. So far, so good.

Satisfied that my setup was good and the water was soothing, I took the scooter back to town. I wanted something besides the busy bees nola bars and I was running out of cherry tomatoes, so I found a Stewart's shop and had a big bowl of chili, despite the heat. I used their bathroom with appreciation, and talked to some Harley riders before going back to my tent site to splash in the river. I drove back to the tent site with more confidence than I would have thought only an hour previously, then went down the tiny embankment and back into the water.

I hadn't brought soap, because even the type labeled biodegradable really isn't good for the water, but I splashed and swam and got my hair wet and felt cooled down and calm. Although the water was not deep there, it was pretty fast, and I was glad it was not deeper, not dangerous. I could see from the flood line that spring brought the water pretty high, at least eight feet higher than it was while I was there, but in the receding water of August it was just right, with little pools connected by flat areas, to splash, rinse my hair, and recharge my own energy. The sun was bright and I decided to rinse out my leggings, hanging them on an old dead tree which hung over the river as if it had been waiting for me.

Once I felt clean and relaxed, I thought it would be pleasant to read in the diminishing sun. I thought it would be nice to be listening to the water on the rounded rocks and watching the sparkles on the water whenever I looked up. It was. It was everything I hoped for, after I made some adjustments.

I didn't have a camp chair, of course, but that was ok, because there were some fallen logs. I could either lean against one or sit upon one. I was fearful of ants so I decided to sit on a log, and that turned out, when I looked down and saw many anthills, to be the right call. For a few pages, I read my paperback happily. I listened to the sound of the bumblebees. There were so many in this fragrant field of wildflowers that I began to marvel that bee populations, worldwide, are in danger. There were so many. And they seemed immense, like a special variety of huge bees, as though they were St. Bernards of bees, the Clydesdales. Luckily I am not afraid of bees, but I did begin to feel as though I were

Camp

My camp

surrounded by them. If I had put down my book and stretched out my hands, I could have swatted bees with both hands at once, which would have been a terrible idea, but it gives an idea how many there were.

I got used to the sound of more bees than I'd ever imagined in my life, and felt peaceful about it, just about when the mosquitoes noticed I was there. At first I swatted them, but they just kept coming, and then I remembered this was fly fishing country, and that there was no way I would keep up with the insects. I had packed good insect repellent, which I put on my skin and my clothes, and, reluctantly, my hair. The greasy feeling of bug spray in my hair was annoying to me, but not as bad as bug bites would have been.

The mosquitoes brought back a memory I had not thought about in many years. I once had a young employee who worked part time while applying to colleges to pursue her real dream: becoming an expert on mosquitoes. She told me that many of the world's diseases could be brought under control if we could just control the mosquitoes, of which there were thousands of varieties.

A foggy morning

I never got the chance to learn more than that, because she got accepted at her dream college into some mosquito study program and I never heard from her again. I hope she reached her dream.

I settled down with my book and heard a sound - something between a crash and a thud. Oh no, the scooter. I had parked it under a tree in case of rain and didn't pay proper attention to the ground, which was sandy. It had fallen over! I had no notion whether I was strong enough to right it again, and I was fearful it had been damaged. Too embarrassed to ask the owners of the inn to come help me, I tried to right it myself, and on the third try I was able to get the scooter upright again, and moved it to a safer, more stable place under the tree. There was a tiny scratch on the front of it but nothing I couldn't get fixed before returning it to its owner. So, having made adjustments to how I would enjoy the riverbank, I did so. I grew to love the sound of the many bees, and how the sound mixed with that of the laughing water. I was amused to see a hummingbird check out my brightly colored tent. I loved the feeling of the sun on my bug spray and sunscreen-covered face.

Clouds were beginning to gather as the sun went down, not a thick cover, but enough for me to think it might rain, so I was glad of the makeshift rain fly but hopeful that it wouldn't be tested.

I loved my little tent and my tent site. Viv didn't mention tenting, but with her adventurous spirit I am sure she would have loved the bumblebee-filled field, and the river, with minnows that happily nibbled at my toes when I went wading. After the sun had set, the planet Venus rose above my tent, and I took one of the happiest photos ever: a planet just above it. I was a little sad that I had to go into the tent to sleep, but it was too cool after the sun went down to sleep outside, and anyway, I didn't want to have to wake up every few hours to apply more bug spray. So, inside it would be, and very cozy it was. I fit perfectly, on the diagonal, and felt rather

A foggy morning pleased at my problem- solving. True, it was cold at first, but many layers, and my own breath, would soon warm the little space. Just as I zipped myself in the tent for the night, a soft but steady rain began, but I was dry and content.

I was content, that is, until I slept. You see, all those hours on the road, when driving the scooter was so unfamiliar to me, did a number on my brain. As I slept, my hands trembled from the grips of the handlebar, and in my dreams the road came at me and at me and at me and no other dreams would come. I woke up uneasy. I read by the camp light for a while, and then, having cleared my brain, was able to sleep blissfully.

It was cloudy and cold when I got up from tenting, and very foggy, which was bad for driving. I splashed around in the river, hoping the fog would lift a little. I didn't get my hair wet, though, because the water, pleasantly cool in the summer sun, was brisk in the morning, and the air at sunrise was too cool for cold water on my skin or hair to be any fun. I didn't like the greasy feeling of last night's bug repellent on my hair, but I would rather bear that than a teeth-chattering swim, and, anyway, my hair would be covered by a helmet most of the day, so I was not worried about how my greasy hair would look.

I broke camp as quickly as I could, dressing in layers for the trip from the camp site to my next expected stop, Schroon Lake. There I hoped to get a good breakfast, my first real meal on the trip. It was terribly, horribly cold as I drove the Honda in the cold fog. I cannot imagine that Viv could have done this trip in October when my teeth were chattering in my three layers in the middle of August.

Still, the fog was pretty, and the slow pace that a scooter necessarily traveled had meant that the fog was not quite as dangerous as it would be in a car. One thing about living in the area most of my life is that I knew that as the sun rose, the views would be beautiful. Pockets of fog, hit by the sun, would be bright, framing the trees and the mountains. This turned out to be the case and made the trip very satisfying as I headed south.

I saw a good many geese on my trip, Canada geese (not Canadian geese; they have no citizenship). Canada geese have straight necks, not the graceful curve of swans or ducks. They are huge. They are also known to be aggressive, and I think they could beat a person to death with those mighty wings. They are only being protective, I know, and I don't blame them for trying to keep their goslings safe or their territory to themselves, but I have been rushed by a goose, and I never want to find out how strong they are. I keep my distance.

At one point, I had to stop entirely, not for fog but for a flock of wild turkeys crossing the road. I can never figure out how one side of the road is better than the other for a wild animal, but there they were, perhaps two dozen of them. I don't fear turkeys the way I do geese, but I didn't want to spook them by driving through the flock, so I was glad to stop and look at them while they chose a different side of the road.

Frontier Town

The remains of Frontier Town were a trip down memory lane for me. In my earliest childhood, my father, a design engineer, was asked for help with the paddle wheel. Success at fixing the problem got our family free admission to Frontier Town for some years. What a thrill that was! It seems incongruous that a wild west theme park was founded and lovingly operated by a Norwegian family, but maybe people outside a culture are able to
Ruins at Frontier Town appreciate it better than those within. (Similarly, I have heard that the world's best living expert on the American Civil War is a Hungarian emigree.) Whatever the reason, Arthur Bensen and family created an old time old west town in the Adirondacks, complete with sawmill, steam train, and bad guys to rob the train.

Ruins at Frontier Town

My husband's family lived in nearby Pottersville, and being also of Norwegian extraction, were friendly with the Bensen family, and when they became old enough, the children of the family got jobs at Frontier Town. My future husband learned to be a good horseman and was so proud of the job that he kept his sheriff's badge, with his name etched on it, until the end of his days.

I loved Frontier Town as a child, and it nags at me that I probably met my husband when I was eleven and he was fifteen and have no memory of it. Those were the glory days of the park. By the time it closed, I was in college. Its closing was sad, but I was OK leaving that part of childhood behind. Frontier Town was revived for a while in the 1980s, and, in addition to the park, they held concerts there. I attended my only Johnny

Cash concert at that property in 1983. My date? My college boyfriend and later husband. So when the chance came to visit the Frontier Town ruins as part of this trip, they held a lot of meaning for me. What memories would this experience trigger?

Maybe memories of my father, who has been gone for many years. When I saw the paddle wheel he designed, would I remember his cleverness? Would it trigger memories of his whole personality, even his bravery? My father fled Hungary in 1956, having been in the uprising on the ethical but losing side. You don't think of your father as a hero. He's just your father. But now I am old enough to be the mother of the brave twenty-something he was, and now I am impressed by his courage. Would I remember more of him, when I saw this childhood place? What about my husband, who worked there when he was a teenager? When I saw the hill where he rode his horse, would it trigger a memory of having met him before I knew I had?

Sadly, none of those memories came to me. I was simply too young when I was first there, and the park was in such ruin I could not place where much of anything had been when I was there. I enjoyed a peaceful rest in the sunshine, at the ruins of the old train station, enjoying everything but remembering nothing.

Between Elizabethtown and Schroon Lake, Route 9 doesn't follow a lake or river the way it does either further north or south, but there was still plenty to see: the tall, ancient pines, some in even rows that showed they had been planted by the Civilian Conservation Corps in the 1930s; the tantalizing trail head signs, for mountains I had neither the time nor the equipment to climb; the abandoned little cabin motels, sturdily standing.

Schroon Lake

I was glad, just the same, to get to Schroon Lake and my expected hot breakfast. Surprise for me, all the diners I had checked out on the way up were closed this Sunday morning. I suppose this may have something to do with this being a town with a heavy church presence. Perhaps it was usual to not have businesses open Sunday mornings. Or maybe these diners had been closed for

A foggy morning in Schroon Lake

COVID reasons, even on my previous trip, but I had not noticed because I didn't stop to eat. I got some coffee and a roll from ubiquitous Stewart's, put a dollar and ninety-eight cents of gas in the tank, parked the scooter, and took a walk to see Schroon Lake.

There are so many lakes in the Adirondacks, each with their own feel, and each so beautiful I am sure that we natives fail to appreciate them. At this part of Schroon Lake, a public gazebo and a beachfront that seemed to be for walking but not swimming welcomed tourists. To the right of the gazebo as you face the lake, Rogers Brook roars through a rocky bed down to the stillness of the larger water. It was very beautiful that morning and I wondered what it would be like to swim in that water. No time that day, though.

Pottersville

After a bit of a worry with a misplaced key, I was back in the saddle and in search of breakfast, which I found at The Black Bear in Pottersville. I am pretty sure the decor has not changed since the 1950s, when it opened, and this suits me fine. The food is the hearty, don't-think-about calories-or-fat, traditional fare of loggers:

The Black Bear Inn in Pottersville

Really good sausages. Abundant eggs. The stools at the counter look as though they belonged in a Norman Rockwell painting and the formica table was the same style my grandmother had in the 1960s, so it triggered a good many memories to be there. The service, the coffee, and the food were all excellent. And there is a taxidermied black bear that you sense roars perpetually while you eat breakfast.

To be in Pottersville is always bittersweet for me. It is where my late husband spent most of his childhood, so he knew it The Black Bear Inn at Pottersville well, but I did not meet him until he had moved to Glens Falls, so it is part of my shared memory, because of my husband's stories, not my real memory. Pottersville is a town that used to be a logging town, used to have its own high school (now Pottersville children are bused to the much larger and better-funded North Warren Central School), but now seems a collection of houses and memories. For a quiet getaway, you can't beat Pottersville.

There was a good deal of money in the second houses logging barons had up north (their main houses might be in Glens Falls or even New York City). You can tell, in the village of Pottersville, that this area used to have some wealth, by the fine architecture and abundant glass in the buildings on the main drag of town.

Natural Stone Bridge and Caves

Natural Stone Bridge and Caves, which is exactly what it sounds like, is a wonderful attraction. The site is that of an old logging camp, but I don't ever remember this place as anything but a tourist site. I'd gone my whole life living near this attraction and had never visited, so I was eager to see if it lived up to the hype, and how it would differ from Ausable Cavern. It's a long and peaceful ride on the side road from Route 9 to the entrance to the caves, and there are signs, similar to the road signs Burma Shave used to use to advertise, on the way. It felt welcoming.

The parking lot was nearly empty when I went in. I was not sure if this was because of COVID or because it was morning, but there was no line when I got my ticket. After I paid, I asked the clerk, a young and energetic woman, if she had a minute to talk. She said she did.

"You know who James Bond is, A cave at Natural Stone Bridge and Caves right?" "Yes." She didn't seem terribly interested, but of course she had to be polite to a customer. "Did you know the author set one of the Bond books

Inviting sign at Natural Stone Bridge and Caves

here in the Adirondacks?" I took out my Pan copy of The Spy Who Loved Me. "See, here's Natural Stone Bridge--right on the cover!"

The clerk was intrigued and called her co-worker over. "Hey, look at this!" "We've got to tell Dee!"

Dee, as it turns out, is the owner, and the business has been in the same family for over a hundred years. The clerks took a picture of the book cover to share with Dee. When I got home, there was a message on my answering machine from Dee, asking how she could get more copies of that book, to give as Christmas gifts to the family.

With a map of the site in hand, I set out on the self-guided tour. The Trout River runs right under the check-in station and gift shop and parking lot, and is still carving out the marble, which is disconcerting when you realize this means it is still carving out rocks under the building you had just been in.

A cave at Natural Stone Bridge and Caves

I should say straight out that the stone bridge is not so much a bridge in the sense of a way to get from one place to another, but a bridge shaped, huge rock, like the front of a cave. If I tell you how big it is, or even show a picture, you can't possibly get the idea of how vast it is. You should just go.

The trails led over rock formations, to an underwater waterfall with a pool. This pool is lovely but the guiding signs warned us about snapping turtles in the water - no swimming! They have snowshoeing treks in the winter, so I hope to be back soon. I also plan to return in the summer, on a trip where I have more time and can go spelunking, and I can't wait to meet Dee.

Warrensburg

Warrensburg is the next sizable town on Route 9 from Pottersville going south. I could have stopped at Chestertown but had a particular thing I wanted to see in Warrensburg, and limited time. In Warrensburg, there is no lake view, but the Hudson River, mighty when it gets to New York City, is a sweet little fast flowing brook that you can wade across in the summer.

I always enjoy following a road by the river and watching The pig bench at Oscar's it become swimmable, then boatable, then mighty. Warrensburg is my usual place to start my river-watching, but the Hudson's origin is in the High Peaks, at Lake Tear of the Clouds. As small as the village of Warrensburg is, it boasts a mighty tourist attraction, Oscar's Smokehouse, famous for its bacon.

Ian Fleming had an obsession with bacon, it seems, working a meal of bacon and eggs or bacon sandwiches into most of his books, and he particularly enjoyed American bacon, insisting in Thunderball that his housekeeper get him some "hickory-smoked American bacon, if we still have some" when he was at the end of a diet. It was convenient for me that the best source of bacon I know was on the way to my next destination.

Oscar's Smokehouse may have the best bacon in the world. Okay, I have not tried all the world's bacon yet, but my parents raised pigs when I was a child, and Oscar's is as good as any we ever had on the farm. Oscar's has been in existence for over one hundred years. I doubt that Ian Fleming ever had Oscar's bacon, even when he was in the area, because in those days before supermarkets he probably enjoyed a product more local to wherever he was staying in Lake George or Glens Falls. But I went to Oscar's not only to enjoy the variety of bacon they offered, but the atmosphere.

Oscar's is romantically set on a hill off Route 9, with a gently winding road that leads to the main building. Sadly,

The pig bench at Oscar's

this is not the original building - really sadly, in fact, because the original building burned down in 2005. When it burned, I was sad to learn it, but surprised to learn that the building lasted as long as it did without a fire, since fire codes for the structure as it was originally built would have been lax by today's standards. The architects were careful, though, and when you go in, you feel taken back, as they say, to a simpler time. The deli case displays the most beautiful cheeses, sausages, and varieties of bacon and other smoked meats. You can get an entire smoked turkey from Oscar's if you are able to pay the price, at this writing about twenty dollars a pound.

And "smoked" is not a monolithic term. Smoked in WHAT? Applewood bacon is different from hickory smoked. In fact, whatever the wood is, it makes a difference. My own favorite is applewood, but wild cherrywood sounds delicious and I hope to try it soon.

I should add that "bacon" in America is different from that of England and Europe. Something happened in the practice of processing meats between the "old" and "new" worlds, and animals are butchered to different patterns. As a result, the same word can be used for a different part of the animal, so that what Americans call bacon is called "streaky bacon" in England, a fattier section of the animal. What people in England call "bacon" is closer to Canadian bacon or ham than what we typically enjoy with our eggs.

I have a friend in England who is an expert on James Bond cooking, and I wanted him to enjoy hickory bacon as Bond did. Even smoked, it won't last indefinitely, so I froze a hunk of hickory-smoked bacon, packed it in ice packs and an Oscar's Smoke House t-shirt, and sent it by express mail. You do not want to know what it cost to send a pound of bacon, wrapped in heavy ice packs, across the ocean. However, it was in my friend's hands in six days, still frozen, and he got his culinary experience.

The back of Oscar's store is more touristy, selling t-shirts, jellies and maple syrup, the sorts of things you'd expect a tourist country store to have. Alas, I could not get any bacon on this day, because I had no place to store it. But I enjoyed the atmosphere, the delectable smells, and the bench on the outside of the store shaped like a plump, happy pig.

Chapter 4

Lake George Area: Sights Ian Probably Saw

Storytown, U.S.A.

On the way to my last place to stay, I passed The Great Escape, now a Six Flags park, once Storytown, U.S.A. Storytown was built in 1954 by Charles "Charley" (not Charlie) Wood, and that date makes it a year older than Disney Land. Mr. Wood started with a few ponies going round in a circle to attract local children. He expanded this to a nursery rhyme themed park about the same time Arto Monaco was doing his Land of Make Believe. As the park became more popular, he expanded it, buying acres and building onto a Class B Wetland, which certainly would not be allowed today. He used the wetland as part of the attraction, though, building a swan boat ride that passed through the swamp, as well as "Jungle Land" with bridges over more acres of swamp. He was resourceful.

He also built two versions of "Gaslight Village." The first was in Pottersville but was moved to Lake George Village in 1958. Gaslight Village boasted old-time attractions such as the "real gas lighting" that Viv mentions, but it was also a really good place for Mr. Wood to store his old car collection, including the original car from the movie Chitty Chitty Bang Bang. There is an Ian Fleming connection, as Ian wrote the children's book on which the movie is based.

Earlier days of Storytown, U.S.A. included little houses designed and built by Arto Monaco, street performers acting out fairy tales, and statues depicting nursery rhymes. I'm old enough to remember sliding down the slide of the huge shoe that was said to have belonged to the old woman of that rhyme.

As Storytown grew, Mr. Wood noticed that the fathers looked bored, so he added "Ghost Town" up on the hill, with an old time train, bank

You can guess who lives here in Storytown

robbery re-enactment, and a saloon where beer was available at an extravagant price. Generations of children helped Sheriff Windy Bill Mckay catch the teenagers playing bandits, and each child got a Storytown deputy badge. Windy did his thing for fifty years and every time I saw him, he seemed as energetic as the first time he ever performed. He was joyful and lively as long as I knew him. There's a monument to him in Ghost Town.

You can guess who lives here in Storytown

As you walk down the hill from Ghost Town back through the park, you will probably miss the tiny bronze statue on "Boot Hill." It is an authentic Remington bronze sculpture of three cowboys riding spirited horses. In its time, Storytown was a repository for the priceless art that Mr. Wood collected, and as an Art History major working my summer job in the park, I would walk around at lunchtime drinking in the purloined letter art, Tiffany windows in a donut shop, priceless bronzes next to shabby wooden grave markers,, gleaming Victorian woodwork decorating gift shops. It still blows my mind that a copy of Porcellino of inestimable value is pawed over by visitors to the Great Escape every day it is open, so that his snout and hooves gleam from the oil of the little hands.

The main house at Wiawaka

Although Charles R. Wood and Ian Lancaster Fleming were both rich men who hung around Lake George in the 1950s, I can find no link between them, no evidence they ever knew each other. Probably their conversation wouldn't have worked out, anyway. Fleming called Storytown a "terrifying babyland nightmare which I need not describe."

Wiawaka

I stayed at Wiawaka as a joke on myself and on the book I was honoring, and my stay there was one of the best nights, and the biggest contrast from my other best night. I went from sleeping on the ground to a beautiful room with an antique cast iron bedstead. I went from granola bars and smooshed fruit to a meal worthy of any caterer. I went from delightfully solo to gratefully in a group.

Staying at Wiawaka was not only a huge contrast to any place I stayed on the trip, it was different from the trip I was typing to recreate. In the book The Spy Who Loved Me, Viv takes her scooter, solo, down Route 9, and happens on a motel which is closing down and stays there for her last few days in the Adirondacks. She is asked by the caretakers to stay there alone one night to wait for the owner, who is scheduled to come get the key the next day. Because it is the 1960s, the phone has been turned off, and because it is the end of tourist season, she is quite alone and doesn't have any expectation that she will see anyone the night before the owner appears. However, this is a James Bond thriller, so horrible gangsters show up, beat and threaten to rape Viv, and intend to burn down the hotel for insurance money, with her in it to take the blame but tell no tale. Luckily for Viv, James Bond shows up and saves the day.

View from the shore at Wiawaka

A great deal of the appeal of Wiawaka, to the modern eye, is its old-fashioned charm. The exquisite old woodwork that can't be made today at any price is in buildings with no air conditioning and no internet, and some of the electric fixtures were visibly routed through old gaslights.

The floor to ceiling mesh of the enclosed porches is another old-time favorite, and the comforting rattle of the windows in the breeze reminds me of my grandmother's house. It is interesting to me that it is the old-fashioned nature that is so seductive now, because when Wiawaka opened in 1903, it must have been a miracle of modern conveniences, such that the women who stayed there

could not have dreamed of: running hot and cold water, showers. gas lighting instead of candles or individual oil lamps, and flush toilets. (In Glens Falls, municipal water was not available to flush waste away until the 1860s, and just because it was available didn't mean everyone had this marvel. The first house I owned, built in 1950, had an outhouse, which was perfectly legal then and there.) To a garment worker of the early 1900s, living in the standard housing of her day and class, staying at Wiawaka must have seemed like a vacation at recently refurbished Four Seasons would to me today. Wiawaka has been in existence since the turn of the last century, and has been running continuously since then, so if our fictional heroine had merely booked a room there instead of taking her chances on an odd Lake George motel, she wouldn't have run into any of that trouble. It was partially a sense of silliness, the absurd idea that a fictional character should have thought things through, that attracted me to Wiawaka. (Although, to be fair, Viv could not have stayed in Wiawaka in October, because the season goes only until the end of August. While the text of The Spy Who Loved Me states the trip is in October, the weather in this book is objectively that of summer, so that is how I justified my stay to myself, in the summer.)

It was partially curiosity that drew me to the site, since, like with Adirondack motels, living in the area, I never saw the need to pay for a hotel where I lived. I could access Lake George, the mountains, and the bike trail just as easily from my house as from Wiawaka, so I never explored the place. However, every Lake George Steamboat trip I have been on, and that has been at least once a year for most of my adult life, the captain includes Wiawaka in his travelogue about great things to see in the area, so I had probably heard of the place dozens of times.

I had missed out on a lot by ignoring Wiawaka all those years. I probably would not have even stayed there for this trip, had I not been cast as an extra in the film Radium Girls, which was filmed at Wiawaka and at various sites in Glens Falls. During the filming, I became charmed by the beauty of the old and carefully constructed buildings and grounds. The filming was in late fall, though, so I had no access to the lake, nor would I want any. The weather during filming was terribly cold, and uncomfortable, but it piqued my interest. I was glad, with the trip, to finally have a good reason to see what it was all about.

I was tired of being on the road, I'll admit it, when I got to Wiawaka. As I took the left turn onto the resort's driveway at the sign saying the great artist Georgia O'Keeffe had stayed there, I longed for and anticipated the uncomplicated rest the place promised, the type of place where artists and writers get things done without distractions.

The parking lot didn't have an obvious place to park a scooter, and, since it looked like rain again, I put the Honda just under a tree, toward the edge of the lot. I left my belongings in the scooter as I walked up to the desk in the main building, Fuller House, to check in.

I went in and found the main desk, "Hello, I am checking in. I am a little early, but could I have my key, please?" The woman behind the desk smiled at this person who obviously had not been there before. "We do not have keys; you just go in your room. What is your name, please?" She found me in the computer record and had me write my name in a paper register. "Will you be eating dinner? Dinner is at six, and breakfast is included, no charge for that, but dinner is fifteen dollars if you'd like it." I elected to pay for dinner, and she took my payment for the room and the extra meal. That was it. No key, no wrist band. She just told me my house and room number, and that my room would be ready at three. I was enchanted by the low-tech vibes, the honesty and the trust of this place.

I was going to be in Mayflower House, a building of Italianate style, with the magnificent large windows, hardwoods everywhere, and detailing. On the porch as you go in is a sign warning that the area is no smoking for restoration reasons. This appealed to me.

Since my room was not ready yet, I dashed home on the scooter and threw my previous few days' laundry in the washer on short cycle, and hung it on the line (who cares if it rains? Final rinse, my mother used to say) before going back to Wiawaka, which gives you an idea how close my own house is to the place. So yes, I could have stayed at home for the final night of my trip. I wanted the opportunity, though, to see Lake George as a tourist might, and I wanted the experience of staying at Wiawaka, which, in their words, "enriches, inspires and celebrates the growth of women." So, after hanging the laundry, getting a change of clothing, and petting my cats, I headed back, and back to the parking spot under the tree.

I was in Room 9 of Mayflower House. I had been in Mayflower House before, sort of. This building was used as the costume shop when filming Radium Girls, and it was a thrill to go back and think, "There's where they kept the dresses! There's where they kept the shoes!" but those things were all on the first floor, and my room was on the second.

At the foot of the stairs was a common refrigerator, and in view of the stairs, a shared bathroom with showers, and I took note of those things for later, but headed up the beautifully curved stairs to find my room. It was quiet, not a lot of people there, almost eerie. The particular scent of old but clean houses filled my nostrils and made me happily remember my grandmother's house.

The thing about Lake George buildings, old ones, anyway, is that not all rooms all face the lake. Before architects learned to design in such a way that everyone got a lake view, they would just build normal houses but on a lake property, which means some rooms are magnificent paradises of lake living and other rooms, well, you could be anywhere, really. As I walked down the hall, I tried to talk myself into liking whatever room I had. I passed a small room. It was charming and cozy, with a lovely old bedstead, but its one window overlooked the parking lot.

Room 9

Would my room face the parking lot? Okay, then I'd be comforted by a view of my scooter. Would it face the garden? Again, I would find that a comfort, and a pretty one. I confess I still hoped to have a lake view. I was astonished when it turned out I did. What luck! Room 9, second floor, Mayflower House, had two small windows, each with a beautiful view through the trees to Lake George. A breeze came in and flowed gently over the first bed. I had been assigned a large room with two twin beds, which, after sleeping in a play tent, seemed unnecessarily luxurious. I sank down onto the bed nearer the lake with gratitude.

At Wiawaka, a bell is rung for all meals at the main house to call people home from the docks and the nature trails and the other buildings. Meals are served buffet style. Everything is laid out in a sensible order. You fill your own plate and take the food to wherever you want to eat. You can go on the porch where big tables await, bring the food to your room, or go down to the docks. Seconds are allowed but sometimes there is a sign asking guests not to take too many of the desserts, for reasons that will shortly be apparent.

Dinner is whatever they decide is for dinner, by which I mean it is not a menu: they make it, you eat it. (If you have allergies or food restrictions and let the kitchen know ahead of time, they will accommodate you.) And what was for dinner that night? Salmon. The most luxuriously prepared salmon, with herbs from the Wiawaka garden, grilled and with a delicate sauce. The squash, or I miss my guess, was also from the garden. The accompanying rolls were so light you practically had to hold them down to eat them, and dessert was delightful New Skete cheesecake.

New Skete cheesecake is a delicacy made by the sisters, Orthodox Christian nuns, of an order in Cambridge, New York. The monastery was founded in 1966, way earlier than The Golden Girls brought attention to cheesecakes. It is actually the monks' monastery located on New Skete Lane, while the nuns are on Ashgrove Road, but they are still the "Nuns of New Skete" because they are associated with the New Skete monastery. In any case, their cheesecakes are both light and rich, and delicately flavored, and if you ever have a chance to try one, eat slowly. Savor it. There is nothing like it. (James Bond connection: You have to pass the New Skete Monastery to get to Black Hole Hollow Farm, which is not only a place where Fleming spent a lot of time, but one he used as the location of the Bond short story "From a View to a Kill.") James Bond would have found this meal delectable. He had a love of fish, and a horror of anything from a freezer, so a meal with local squash and delicately herbed salmon would have seemed just right. The sensuous dessert made by nuns would have evoked one of Bond's great double entendres. Wiawaka does not serve alcohol but you are permitted to have it on site (although not at table), so Viv probably would have enjoyed a whiskey in her room, or down at the dock after the sun went down.

I enjoyed the company of the other women staying at Wiawaka, while we ate our luscious meal on the big screened porch. I particularly enjoyed this dinner itself because this was my first sit-down dinner in days. Even a bowl of cold cereal, at a table, would have made a satisfying evening meal at that point, but a real

A dip at Wiawaka -a perfect way to start the day meal with courses, and plates and tableware seemed a luxury.

After dinner, I headed to the dock for a swim. There is more than one swimming area at Wiawaka, each roped in but with no lifeguard, so guests are told to swim at their own risk but to please stay in the ropes. Swimming in Lake George is a different experience each day you do so, even in different parts of the same day. Waves can be three feet high in the afternoon, but in early morning and early evening the lake tends to be smooth, and my after-dinner swim was of the smooth and relaxing variety.

A dip at Wiawake -a perfect way to start the day

After dinner, I could have hung out with my dinner companions, but I wanted sleep. I wanted rest, and I wanted a bed, and no bed ever felt as welcoming as the twin bed under the window of Room 9, Mayflower House. For a while, I heard the music from a band playing at a bar across the lake. I liked it.

There was a time this would have annoyed me, but there had been no night life for many months of COVID, so the idea of people making merry made me happy, too. And really, the music didn't go on all that late. After the music ended, I could still see some lights twinkling from the village, and they were beautiful and far off, and where I was it was still and marvelously dark.

In the morning, I was up before the sun. The room was quiet, as was the house. A light had been left on in the hall, but it was not bright, and, having grown up in the country, I remembered how dark it would be outside with no lights if I went to the dock. If you have grown up in the woods, though, you probably learned how to walk so as to feel roots and rocks without tripping on them. I pulled on some shorts and a shirt and went down the softly lit stairs, barefoot so as to feel my way. Then I was where it was darker, then away from the house, down to the dock where the dark was real.

I had been taking pictures on my phone for the whole trip, but left the phone in my room. Frankly, the phone was nearly useless at Wiawaka. Internet only worked in the main building. And I wanted to enjoy the morning darkness. I didn't want to take photos of the lights of Lake George Village, across the lake, or even of the sunrise. I just wanted to enjoy the morning, be in the moment, so, no phone.

As I walked down the hill to the dock, I saw a large shadow, a darker bit of dark. Faintly, I could see the silhouette of a deer. I stood still. I was worried I would frighten the creature, but the deer stood looking at me, unafraid. We stood there, silently, for some time. I could hear the deer's even breathing, not the snorting that says fear. It was some other crash in the darkness that set the deer bounding away.

I briefly wished I had brought my phone, but perhaps the motion of my taking it from my pocket would have frightened the deer and I would not have had those magical moments in its company. In any case, I share with you the peaceful time the deer and I just stood there, looking at each other, before dawn on an August morning. It was lovely.

I went down to the dock and realized I should have put on my bathing suit instead of pulling on shorts and a t-shirt because the air was still and warm and the water almost the same temperature, my favorite conditions for swimming. But no one was up, anyway, so I pulled off my clothes and got into the water, walking in instead of diving because it was an unfamiliar place to swim. (I have known two friends who broke their necks diving into unfamiliar water, so I am cautious.)

If you have ever been skinny-dipping, you know the water glides over you in a way you can't imagine while wearing a bathing suit. It was a lovely experience! The water was cool, the darkness welcoming, and there were no bugs. What a contrast to a few nights before, swimming in the Boquet in the hot sun. After a while, I walked to the dock to drip dry before putting my clothes back on. I sat next to my clothes and I took in my surroundings. Southwest, across the lake, the lights of Lake George Village could be seen, bright here and there but not oppressively so.

Lake George, early morning

In the sky, stars glistened, lightly veiled by wispy clouds. I listened to the lapping of the water on against the dock, and marveled that the sound of lapping could occur when the lake seemed so smooth, as it usually does in the morning. I sat and I listened, content. The sun began to rise, the light of the sun making the eastern sky pink, and it seemed interesting to me, the blackness of the southwest view of the village with intense dots of light, contrasting with the smooth darkness to the north and east, softly and smoothly gaining color. At this point, I was dry enough to put my clothes back on. The sky was half-pink when I headed back to the house. Before breakfast was served, I headed out to the Holy Grail of my journey, the site of the motel in the book I was recreating. Many James Bond book locations are real places, which added to the authenticity of the writing. Fleming even stated on numerous occasions that he could not write about places he had not been. But this broad statement of his isn't entirely accurate; Fleming was writing fiction, and like many fiction writers, sometimes had to move things around geographically, for plot reasons.

The location of the actual motel will never really be found, because there was no single Dreamy Pines Motel. There was no Dreamy Pines Motel in Lake George, early morning the City Directory of Glens Falls or of Lake George at that time. There were, and still are, dozens of bucolically named summer places: Tall Pines. Twin Birches. The Pines. Whispering Pines. But no Dreamy Pines, and no lake called Dreamy Waters, although we have Trout Pond, Mud Pond, Lake Desolation (my favorite) and Forest Lake.

It becomes more maddening because Fleming wrote over a dozen times that Dreamy Pines is south of Lake George on Route 9, but in an inexplicable turn, once had the heroine say it was west of Lake George. There are no communities now, and certainly none in 1960, due west of Lake George, The western location of Dreamy Pines would be easier to ignore if it were not on the first page of the book. On the second page, and every page thereafter, Dreamy Pines is south of Lake George.

Actually, were it not for that weird mistake on the first page, the location of the imaginary hotel might be possible to pinpoint. Viv gives specific directions. She is headed south on Route 9 and says she takes the turnoff right past Storytown, U.S.A., and that this side road leads to an alternate route between Lake George and Glens Falls, a route not quite as busy as Route 9. This puts her on Round Pond road, and names "Dreamy Waters" as a stand in for Round Pond, and fixes the "alternate route" as Bay Road. I was glad for the early morning and its quiet peace as I set out to make the very turn that Viv did. By this time, I had become a skilled and confident scooter driver, no longer as afraid of traffic. I wanted the quiet, though, because I sought to enjoy the peace and solitude, and because, once at the turn, I was to make a video to post to my followers on Twitter. For that I would need the quiet of morning. Even 8:30 am would be too late, on Route 9 in August, for a quiet video. This was rather Viv's point, that she left Route 9 on purpose, for peace. It was the opposite of peace that she got when she found that cabin on the little lake, but unexpected turns are what makes any story good.

I kicked up a little gravel as I left the driveway of Wiawaka and headed west on the winding road to Route 9. Unlike Viv, I enjoyed the sight of the pines and although I couldn't hear much over the buzz of the scooter, I could see the branches moved by the wind, with what I knew was a whispering sound.

I got to Storytown, now The Great Escape. I parked at a now-closed restaurant across the street. I put my phone in the holder to record the moment. Back on the road, I signaled my left turn, and set off to make the turn. There was a thrill running through me as I left Route 9, and it sustained as I drove toward Round Pond. I checked the video, but because of the scooter's engine noise, it was not quite what I wanted, so I made another one, just holding the phone, but showing "Storytown," the main route, and the turnoff. Then I headed to Round Pond to take photos of the privately-owned cabins that still stand there.

Locals have variously told me, each with great confidence, that Dreamy Waters is at Round Pond, at some Lake George Motel or other, or even in Bolton Landing. Ivar Bryce says, in his memoirs, that Dreamy Waters is between Cambridge, New York, and Glens Falls, and it seems there was a motel on that route that physically resembled the layout of Dreamy Pines. However, Round Pond is the only location that matches the text of the book. As I paused at Round Pond, the terrain also matched the book. The pines were as they should be. I took photos as the sun rose, and I felt good. I headed back to Wiawaka and didn't have to wait long for someone to come out and strike that silver bell that told us a meal was served. It was hard to wait even a short time for breakfast at eight. When you are up before the sun and the sun rises at five, that's a long time to wait. Luckily, I had one or two more granola bars left, and guests are allowed to help ourselves to coffee in the main building at any time of day or night. Coffee and granola tided me over until the meal was served.

Breakfast was magnificent. The main breakfast entree was enchiladas. I had never thought of enchiladas as a breakfast meal, but they were well-seasoned, hearty but not too filling for morning. If a guest didn't want an enchilada, or if she was hungrier than that, there was a variety of breakfast cereals, oatmeal (the sign said "real oatmeal," meaning they would prepare it for you instead of your pouring hot water over a packet of instant), bagels you could toast, real cream cheese, rolls, fresh cut melons, berries, oranges and apples, and perfectly hard boiled eggs.

I had sufficiently rested so that I looked forward to company, and joined a table full of peppy morning people discussing books. We talked about how much we enjoyed Wiawaka and what we intended to do that day. Mostly, the women with whom I shared the table were going to enjoy one another's company and take in the joys of Wiawaka. There were no programs scheduled, but there was swimming and an abundance of nature trails.

After seeing the possible location of the motel in The Spy Who Loved Me, my goal that day was to see the village of Lake George as much as a tourist would as I could, and to go on a steamboat ride because Viv liked steamboats, which should be no surprise since James Bond is often on a boat of one size or another. I had packed a sun hat when I briefly went back to my house, and a sweater, since experience has taught me that, no matter how hot the summer day is, it will be chilly on the deck of a boat on the lake. I clothed myself in a cotton dress with leggings beneath, packed my sun hat in the milk crate, and set out for the day.

One of the things that cements me as the town character is that I wear wide-brimmed hats most of the year. I have done this since High School, when sunscreens were not as effective as they are now, when no one wore a hat except as a costume, but when I had an obsession with Morticia Addams and wanted to stay pale. One of the advantages of approaching little-old-ladyhood is that it is no longer seen as unusual to be wearing a broad-brimmed hat. Someone once said to me, "I saw you downtown yesterday, but you were too far away to say hi, but then it turned out it was just another woman in a great big hat." I treasure that comment. Anyway, my straw hat, safely at the bottom of the milk crate, would spring back into shape when I put it on, and I set out to find parking confident that my hat was there for me.

Lake George Village

Lake George Village now has electronic parking meters. Parking meters, by the way, were invented during the Depression, which is the biggest municipal salt-in-the-wound I can think of. As a local, I believe it is a matter of pride to not pay for my parking, so I drove up to the side streets, to the trailhead for Prospect Mountain, where the meters do not exist and where there is blessed shade. The shade was not so important on the scooter, but on the days I drive a car to Lake George, I try to park under a tree so I will not come back to a suffocating bubble of steamy air and nasty hot seats. I found my usual spot under a maple tree waiting for me, exchanged my helmet for the hat, tied my sweater around my waist, and was off to the boat. It was a lovely walk down the hill from the quiet of the trailhead to the bustle of the village.

The description of maples and pines are a striking part of The Spy Who Loved Me. Fleming loved the vivid red of maples in autumn. In his manuscript, though, he called the red trees

A sign in the Village of Lake George

"sycamores." I read his earliest typescript, which is housed in Lilly Library in Indiana, and was puzzled by the reference to sycamores. I had no idea what a sycamore was, what it looked like, where they lived. When I got around to looking it up, I found that the shape of sycamore leaves is similar to that of maples, but that sycamores tend not to have the eye-catching colors. My guess is that Fleming saw the shape of maple leaves when he was visiting the area and assumed they were his familiar sycamore, and that someone in the editing process corrected him to maples.

I find maples beautiful year-round even though I am almost deathly allergic to their pollen. In the spring, their leaves are the most perfect pale green, and the flowers the same, and when the flowers fall on a breezy spring morning it is as if it is everyone's wedding day. The darker green of summer (dark purple for some imported trees) on heavier leaves make the limbs sway rather than bob when the wind is blowing lightly in a way I find comforting.

Entire businesses have sprouted up making money from the glory of the autumn color, and in the winter, the shape of a maple tree is pleasing, like a giant outstretched hand. Maples are not the only tree in the Adirondacks, but it makes sense to me that they get so much glory.

Fleming, and his heroine, Viv, disliked pine trees, and I am not sure which types she is talking about. She says you "can't shelter under them or climb them, and they are covered with the most un-treelike black dirt." There are so many varieties of pines, and some you can climb, although it is a prickly experience, but if you can neither climb nor shelter, she may be referring to

Caring for our four-legged friends

scrub pines, whose rather ungraceful shape makes them unwelcoming for climbing and which have thick and stubborn pitch. But they smell lovely, and Viv allows that the scent of pine is so wonderful that "when I can afford it" she gets pine essence for her bath. My guess as to the type of "pine" in the book is plain white pine, because the needles are long and soft, and match the needles described by James Bond when he used them for hair in a dummy he made of himself to confuse the bad guys.

As I walked down the hill from where I parked, the trees were fewer and the view of the lake became better, and I tried to see the village with fresh eyes. It isn't easy to see a place you have been all your life as a tourist would, but I tried. I tried to imagine what this would feel like, had I never been here, but the childhood A sign in the Village of Lake George memories were so delightful it was difficult to push them away, and the more I tried, the more appeared. I remembered the wonders of Lake George Village when I was a child, how wonderfully lit up it was, how the many shops enchanted me. In those days, my family would go through the village just for the pleasure of seeing the summer traffic cops. With sleek uniforms resembling those of beat cops, bright white gloves, and silver whistles, the young men (always men) kept order in the crazy summer tourist traffic. The village didn't see any reason at that time, I guess, to invest in traffic lights when there was no traffic to speak of nine months of the year. I am told the traffic cops worked for gym credits at colleges. I remember one young man who came back for several years in a row, who danced as he pointed and lightly blew the whistle to let the drivers know when to stop and when it was safe to go. I miss him. I miss the traffic cops, who were surely there when Ian Fleming was in the area. I

The map of Lake George

Caring for our four-legged friends made my way through a Lake George village that was loud and crazy fun, but controlled by traffic lights.

Did you know that "nostalgia" in its earliest uses meant an unhealthy longing for the past? It's the "algia" ending (neuralgia, fibromyalgia) meaning "pain" that is the tip off. Not everything in the past is better. Sometimes change can be wonderful. One thing I love about now is that we put bowls of water out for the dogs that visit the area. I lost count of the number of Lake George village businesses that welcome our quadruped friends. Thankfully there has been some change, since the 1960s, in the view of Native Americans. No longer do shops have items "for little Indians" and fake headdresses that wouldn't have been a part of the culture in this area, anyway. Sadly, the occasional out of place, out of time period "Indian" statue still exists. In an appalling lack of insight, a monument at Fort William Henry still tells a story of "hostile Red Indians." We have made improvements in our views, but still have a long way to go toward treating Native Americans with respect.

The more things change, the more they stay the same. The business names may be different from my childhood and from when Ian Fleming was in the area, but we still have fast food, t-shirts in questionable taste, shops with "souvenirs' imported from China. The names have changed since my childhood, but the vibe is the same.

It was a little sad to go to the site of the old Gaslight Village. It's a park now; I seem to remember that at one point a sign identified that Gaslight Village had been there, but now, just a park. In my lifetime, the amusement park once owned by Charles R. Wood had gone from an old-timey themed park with antique cars (including Chitty Chitty Bang Bang), stage and ice shows in a theater called the Opera House, and an "old tyme" photo booth, to a typical fun park with modern but predictable carnival rides to a nature park and a playground for children under twelve. It is a delightfully designed place with paths that lead from a climbing place to a spot

The map of Lake George to make music and more. And it's free.

Then again, not all the businesses have changed. While Dr. Morbid's Haunted House has recently closed, at this writing the wonderfully silly House of Frankenstein still welcomes those who want an old time scare. There are multiple miniature golf courses, including one said to have been frequented by the artist Georgia O'Keeffe.

On the main drag, Capri Pizza still has the best calzones it has ever been my pleasure to try. Until June of 2022, Howard Johnson's - the last such restaurant in the entire world! - still welcomed A rose from the garden diners to eat

A rose from the garden

under its famed orange roof, but now, sadly, is closed. Probably my favorite sight in all of Lake George Village besides the lake itself is the model, in concrete, of the lake. This area of blue, about thirty-two feet long, shows the distinctive shape of the lake, and marks where the towns are on its shores. Visitors and locals alike have their pictures taken standing on this lake model, with the real lake behind them. Benches and chairs in the relaxed Adirondack style circle the model for viewers to rest or to wait their turns to be photographed. And just behind this model is the most wonderful, three-season flower garden.

I don't know what proportion of the flowers in the garden are native, although I imagine it is few. Surely the Rosa Rugosa that makes up so much of it is not native. However, the beautiful color and scent of this rose make it a delight to the senses. The Rosa Rugosa is as hardy as the wild rose native to our area and thrives at temperatures that can go from negative forty degrees Fahrenheit to over one hundred degrees. The rugosa's scent is sweet and strong, also resembling that of the native wild rose. However, the rugosa presents its beautiful flowers for months at a time, while the wild roses produce only in June. The rugosa of the Lake George garden is joined by lilies, echinacea, and other plants I didn't identify, and by signs saying "Please don't pick the flowers."

The Cruise

A gift shop in Lake George Village

The heroine of The Spy Who Loved Me dislikes the village of Lake George. She calls it "honkytonk" and "gimcrack." But she likes Fort William Henry ("the stockade fort") and the boats "steamboats that ply their way to Ticonderoga." While I didn't quite have time to take the boat all the way up to Ticonderoga, I wanted a longer ride than the Minne Ha Ha's hour-long cruise, so I had booked the lunch cruise on the Lac du St. Sacrament.

The Mohican is the only one of the current Lake George steamships Ian Fleming could possibly have sailed on, since it is the only one still operating that was in existence in 1960; in fact, it has been on the water since 1908. Whenever I am on the Mohican, my favorite boat because of its age, I marvel that it is twice the size of the

Mayflower. I cannot imagine crossing the entire ocean in a boat so small, and I feel crowded even standing around with two hundred people, and it blows my mind to think of having to sleep and eat in such a crowded place for over a month.

My trip would not go as far as across the ocean but would go at least to Bolton Landing, where we could see the magnificent Sagamore Resort. This magnificent hotel is not in The Spy Who Loved Me, but it seems to have been mentioned, tongue in cheek, in another Fleming thriller, Diamonds Are Forever. In Diamonds Are Forever, James Bond stays at a motel called the Sagamore in Saratoga Springs. It is a sorry place, though, and Bond finds it shabby--a good joke for anyone who has ever stayed in the place of the same name in Bolton LandA gift shop in Lake George Village ing. It is interesting that Fleming has two rather nasty motels in two separate books, because in a 1962 interview for a Long Island newspaper, Fleming had said, "I sometimes stay in motels, and I love them." Known by locals as the "Saint," the Lac du St. Sacrement is the newest of the Lake George steamships. I found it necessary to break my own rule about doing only things the book's heroine could have done, here, because the Mohican, which is old enough for Ian's heroine to have seen it, doesn't have long cruises and she specifically refers to a longer one. The Saint, launched in 1989, is well known for its dinner cruises, jazz nights, fireworks Cruises. I should have figured out, since the Saint is known for "champagne cruises," that I was in for something special.

I'd never been on the lunch cruise and hadn't paid much attention to their advertising, so I figured "lunch" meant a bagged sandwich and a piece of fruit. I was in for a surprise, and I got the idea that this was something more than a bag lunch as I was still in line to board. The workers in officer's uniforms asked "Lunch, or cruise only?" and put us in different lines accordingly. Once on the boat, I was greeted formally by a young woman in a bright white shirt and black pants who took me to my own private table. I should mention that my usual Lake George Steamboat experience is the Minne Ha Ha's hour-long cruise. It's wonderful. We get to hear the calliope, go down to steerage and see the workings of the paddle wheel, and enjoy historical narration, all in an hour. It's lovely, but the seats are first come, first serve, and even if you leave your sweater on a chair to indicate it is yours, if you leave for even a few minutes, your prime chair may be taken by someone else who liked the view from that vantage point.

I couldn't have picked a better day for my trip, sunny with just a few clouds, and I was pleased that I had my hat for the sun, and my sweater for the wind. Turns out neither was strictly necessary, because my table was in a glassed-in area at the prow of the boat. Just like I chanced into the best room at Wiawaka, I chanced to the best possible table on the Saint.

Or maybe it was not chance, in either case. Maybe, because of COVID, there were few enough people traveling that I just got a good seat because the boat was not yet full. And, actually, any seat at all would have been nice. Every table was covered with a white tablecloth, and the silverware and glassware (not plastic!) gleamed. My waiter introduced herself and told me this was my seat for the entire trip.

When I sat down, I put my hat, superfluous for now, on a windowsill, rather than on the table. Time was I would have felt self-conscious, sitting at a table for two by myself. By the time of this trip I had been widowed for over ten years and long ago resigned myself to the fact that there are many things which, if I want them enough to experience them, I will enjoy them on my own. I didn't feel the sting of many eyes on me as I sat on the Saint, and then again, they didn't treat me oddly for being by myself. Hosts at restaurants often look over my shoulder for the other person when they ask, "How many?" but here the person had taken my ticket, consulted the signup sheet and seen I was by myself, and seated me without comment. It was nice.

It is possibly the solo nature of James Bond books that appeals to me, especially as I get older. Bond has meaningful interactions with some people, but, more often, he just natters to himself about what he is doing, or has done, or is planning to do. Much of the appeal of Bond books is in paragraph after paragraph of Bond taking pleasure, by himself, in a fine meal, beautiful view, or the wonder of wildlife, especially birds. As I sat by myself at the table, I thought about the love of the great outdoors present in every Bond book, present just as much as his love of cars and ships. And naturally I had to take the time to look over the boat. It truly is a beauty! A dance floor that looks like real hardwood on the deck below my own. A gently curved staircase to get there. Sleek lines, a modern, spacious bathroom, the Saint has everything to make you feel as though you are traveling in

Dance floor of the Lac du St. Sacrement

comfort and deserve to.

Well, that's on the paid-for-lunch side. On the other side, it is still a sleek and gleaming ship, but with chairs that slide around with a horrible squeak as the legs scrape the bare deck, placed closely together so that there's bound to be "Excuse me, excuse me" as you try to get past the chairs for a view of the lake. On the lunch side, people dressed accordingly. On the cruise-only side people tended to wear the shorts and t-shirt uniform usual for summers at the lake, and the outfit that I often wear as well. Even from the dock, even so close to the village, you can see the trees that have been undisturbed for hundreds, or thousands of years, stretching up the height of a mountain. As close to the village as the dock, old houses can be seen that dot the east side of the lake, houses that if they were in a city, and not on a lake, would be worth ten percent of

Parasailers are a familiar sight above Lake George

their value on the water. On the village side, the view is of a good deal of concrete, of another dock, of the rebuilt fort, brown logs looking warm and oddly inviting, its old battlefield now a park with, more than likely, picnickers and families throwing frisbees. Looking at Lake George itself, I could see sailboats, and motor boats. Not a lot of jet skis on that day. The wind made the lake choppy, beyond the dock, with waves not at their highest, Parasailers are a familiar sight above but little white waves as if they Lake George were practicing for how high they could be, later. Near the shore, at what is

Lake George Village, as seen from the boat

informally called "Dog Beach," a man in waders was fishing. I could also see several parasailers, high and bright against the blue and white of the summer sky.

Parasailing terrifies me. I have a low tolerance for risk. People think I have a high tolerance for risk because of the things I do for fun: motorcycling, hiking, pole dancing, roller blading, scuba diving. But if you take a look at each of these activities, you can see that they are things that require skill and commitment on the part of the person doing them. The person doing them is, to a large extent, responsible for how safe these activities are. For example, you can't (or at least it is difficult) be

Lake George Village, as seen from the boat a motorcyclist without getting a license that ensures you have some skill. For SCUBA you need to get trained and certified. In parasailing, all the risks are out of the hands of the person doing the activity. I would have no way of knowing how to check the harness for safety, and I would have to depend on the person who selected the harness to ensure it is the right one, to make sure it was in good working condition. Once up in the air, I would have to hope the person running the business knew how to bring me down safely. No, thank you. I will say, though, that parasailing is beautiful. I love to see the huge, brightly colored parachutes as other people, braver than I, enjoy the lake from one hundred fifty feet above it. It's not for me, but it gives me pleasure that other people enjoy this.

My daughter rolls her eyes when I say I have a low tolerance for risk. "Mom, what about Jamaica? What about the lagoon?" She likes to remind me of the time we were in Jamaica and I gave a man two hundred dollars to take us for a moonlit swim in a "luminous lagoon" where microorganisms glow at your touch. She reminds me that I didn't know that man, that he put a half dozen people unknown to each other in a rickety van, took us to a dive bar where we were all given rum drinks and then put us on a boat going through waters unknown to us where we were expected to jump in with no life jackets, as an example of risky behavior. But I can explain. I think. My best friend says that on my tombstone, whenever I die, whatever I die of, the appropriate caption will be, "She was always pulling sh!t like this." Before the boat even left the dock, we passengers were encouraged to get our lunches and drinks. I ordered a seltzer but noted the drink prices were reasonable for summer in a holiday town. The food selection was vast. On the way to the buffet was a soup and bread station. I viewed this as an excellent idea in crowd control, thinning out the group by having a good proportion of them start with the soup. A little farther on was the meal proper, with a selection of salads, rolls, baked pasta entries, baked meat entrees, and just past that a carving station with ham, beef, and turkey. I am not vegetarian or vegan but enough of my friends are that I pay attention to such things, and had I been vegan I would not have gone hungry. The salad contained no croutons, I noted, good for people who cannot have gluten.

Out on the deck

I helped myself to salad (romaine, not iceberg) and bread (white, whole grain, and rye were available) and fresh fruit, and moved on to the carving station. The carver was deaf, and a printed paper sign indicated that we point to the meat we wanted, and she would help us. This moved smoothly.

The only sign language I know is "thank you" so I did that sign and got an answering sign. Back at my table, I took a picture of my meal, Instagram style, before beginning to eat, and as I began, the boat began to pull away from the dock.

Just before we began our journey, the Captain's voice came on the speakers, "There will be three loud blasts as we pull away from the dock. Small children will want to cover their ears." And it's true; as a child the blasts were painful, but years of too much sound have made it so that the blasts are loud, but no longer hurt.

I have never yet been on a Lake George cruise that didn't have these two qualities: Excellent narrative content, and terrible audio quality. I've gotten so I accept, even embrace, the bad audio quality the same way you accept that your beloved great uncle will always misuse some characteristic vocabulary word. At this time in my life a Lake George cruise narrative is a great deal like a beloved uncle's stories, because in over fifty years I have heard them, well, over fifty times: Lake George is about thirty-two miles long. It is landlocked, and, at points, up to two hundred feet deep. Adirondack means "they eat bark," more or less, a comment from one native group to another. Minne Ha-Ha means

Wiawaka from the water

"laughing waters." We drink the water right from the lake, so please don't litter.

The first white man to see what we now call Lake George was Isaac Jogues, that missionary who called it Lac du St. Sacrament, or, the Lake of the Blessed Sacrament. Lake George is called "The Queen of American Lakes," and is considered one of the most beautiful bodies of water in the world.

Those above points I just rattled off, without having to look them up. I love this.

After I finished my meal, I went up on deck, and strained to hear the audio, but mostly I knew when to tune in, when to really pay attention. The wind was brisk but not really cold, and not so fierce as to remove my hat from my head.

I've gotten so I look forward to particular points of interest: There's Wiawaka, where I was staying, and where tired, under-paid women from the garment industry got a chance to rest, starting in the early twentieth century.

There's the Peabody House--the very garment industry that was exploiting them. There's an island you can camp on--call the 800 number, answered by someone in California who is unable to recommend a site and knows nothing about them, to reserve. There's the Grace Memorial Chapel, designed by the same man who designed Carnegie Hall, which looks so precarious on its own little island.

And, more recently, "If you look to your left, you can see a bald eagle on the top of that pine. Bald eagles are making a comeback since . . . "and how wonderful that is! I remember being a young child and my environmentalist mother (only at that time they called it "the ecology movement") lamenting that DDT had made it impossible for predatory birds to hatch their eggs. I never thought, at that time, that I would see an eagle in my entire life, and now, on a boat ride near a populated area, we can see two in quick succession. I joined the other bird watchers on the port side of the boat, straining, and succeeding in seeing a still, majestic bird at the top of a scrub pine. The white feathers of the head were bright in the sunshine, and I could see why they were called "bald." I wondered how the captain was so sure the bird would be there, that it would not fly away as we passed. The bird just sat there, though. The eagle on the next island did that, too. I don't know what I expected them to do, but they just sat there. I guess I am used to seeing songbirds at my bird feeder, where the little birds dart around, or the blue jays that bring each other gifts of pieces of popcorn or fruit, or even crows that talk to each other for a long time. I have seen hawks, gliding, circling; I've marveled at the impossibly slow wing sweep of noble herons, and I have seen crows desperately trying to escape the more

The Sagamore from the summit of Buck Mountain, October

maneuverable sparrows. I have by now seen eagles several times, but all they did was sit there, which, at least, allowed me to get a photo of a gleaming white head. I am told that eagles eat fish, so perhaps they sit for that long while waiting for just the right fish to be in the shallow waters near the island. Or maybe they were hatching eggs, now that they can do so.

I loved being on deck, as I always do, listening to the swoosh of the water and the rumble of the engines, watching the boats on the lake and the birds in the sky. As we headed north, people on the shore and in smaller boats waved at us, another Lake George tradition, and I happily returned the greetings.

As usual, when on the lake, I marveled at its power and danger. I'm a strong swimmer but I know that, if I fell off the boat in the middle of the water, I would die of exhaustion before I could swim to shore, that is, if I didn't get run over by a motor boat. It also amazes me that water we can swim in becomes water we can walk on only a few months later. I have friends in England and I used to envy their temperate climate. They have lower heating bills and don't have to buy outfits for temperatures that range from below zero Fahrenheit to approaching one hundred degrees. But that also means that for my English friends it never The Sagamore Hotel at Bolton gets

The Sagamore Hotel at Bolton

warm enough to swim or cold enough to ice skate. I would miss that.

The Saint was to turn around just before the opulent Sagamore. White, bright, looking as crisp as a new shirt, this hotel dominates the little island it inhabits. Even from far away you can see the porticos and the immense dock. If you are lucky, you may see the Sagamore's own boat, The Morgan, headed out for the day. The Sagamore is so large and so stunningly white that it can easily be seen by hikers who have made it to the summit of Buck Mountain. Buck Mountain is clear across the lake, and its elevation is over two thousand feet, and I have taken fine photos of the Sagamore from Buck's summit.

Many locals are employed at the Sagamore, with the usual resort paradox that the people who work there couldn't possibly afford a night's stay. Mostly, the Sagamore is too rich for my blood as well, although being unable to stay there doesn't mean I was never in the area. When I had just gotten my scuba certification, I remembered that guests dropped things off the dock by mistake. The law as I understood it at the time was that you couldn't trespass on private property by land, but that any approach by boat could get you, legally, within a few feet of the dock. So, my scuba partner and I would set out from Bixby Beach, at that time a public boat launch (at this writing it is closed and I doubt it will ever re-open) in a small boat with an outboard motor, and dive from the boat, near the dock. The lake bottom was very silty there, but we were able to find glassware, teacups, saucers, and several fishing poles. We didn't have any use for multiple fishing poles and tried to return them to the Sagamore, but the person we talked to just looked at us as though we were crazy, so we felt a lot better about keeping the glassware.

I learned to scuba in Lake George, and I recommend it. A pool can't prepare you for the experience of currents and fish the way a lake can. And while I have been diving in Lake Luzerne, the Hudson River, the Sacandaga, and the Bahamas, Lake George is my favorite.

There is nothing to compare for the thrill of reaching that first thermocline (the spot where the temperature of the water takes an abrupt dive) and knowing you are ready for it. Freshwater fish are not as bright as those in the Caribbean, but depending on where you go, they can be curious, even friendly. The vibrating sound of boat motors, when you are listening to this under the water, is weirdly soothing. I love the outer space feeling of being underwater, especially in Lake George, where the sand, and then the rock, stretches out before you and sometimes it is difficult to know which way you are facing.

There was only one other woman besides myself in my scuba class, and we both nearly failed on the first day. We kept falling over. Like most pleasurable skills, from ballet to driving a car,

The sparkling water of Lake George

you have to get good at the boring stuff before you can do anything even remotely interesting, so on the first day our initial job was to kneel in shallow water, fully equipped in our gear.

The other woman in the class, named Beata, was, like me, short and small, but the instructor didn't think it was our small size that was the problem, as he had instructed short men before. He'd never instructed any women, though. Beata and I tried and tried, through sheer force of will, to stay up-right, but time after time we fell over in the water. I thought maybe it was our higher center of gravity that was making us less stable. The instructor was speculating that maybe women just can't do scuba. But Beata and I knew that women have become divers, and so we searched ourselves for the reason.

The problem, as it turns out, was modesty. Women are taught from earliest girlhood to keep our legs together, no matter what. "Don't let the boys see your pretty underpants," toddlers are told. "Don't spread your legs, not even under the desk," schoolgirls hear. Women get so used to keeping our legs together that Beata and I hadn't even noticed we were doing it, or that the men were not. Once we brought our legs apart, straddling imaginary horses as the men had been doing, we were as upright as any of them. Viv does not mention scuba diving, but James Bond does this a great deal. The underwater sequences in the books can be terrifyingly vivid, or poetically beautiful, and as a diver I'd say, even though the equipment has changed, Fleming gets the feel of it right.

It is a shame that the organization Bateaux Below was not yet founded when Ian Fleming was in Lake George, since, with his fascination with things to do with the Revolutionary War, he might have worked something into The Spy Who Loved Me. There are multiple boats (bateaux) in relatively shallow waters available for even beginning divers to see. Every Lake George boat ride the captain mentions that the boats would be sunk by one army to keep them from getting in the hands of the other, and that later the intent was to raise them and reuse them, and every boat ride I wonder how they intended to get the boats before scuba was invented.

The Saint turned around just before the Sagamore and headed south, mostly hugging the opposite shore, so this time the sites were Wiawaka, the Monastery where they raise German Shepherds, which is tied to the Nuns of New Skete, a few carefully deOregano signed houses (one with a miniature Statue of Liberty) and acres and acres of trees that look much as they would have hundreds of years ago. I never get tired of the unsullied trees, or of the sparkle on the water in the afternoon sun, like so many dancing crystals.

Oregano

As I left the boat, the photographers showed me the prints of the photo they had taken when I got on. Uncharacteristically, I bought the package. I later sent the prints to the people who most generously sponsored the trip. If I hadn't had the sponsors, I still could have done it--sort of. I would not have been able to afford a good set of motorcycle gloves, a stay at glorious Wiawaka, or entrance to the historical sites without sponsorship. I hope that they liked the photos.

It was with real sorrow that I left

Wiawaka. I felt more relaxed, happier, more myself there than I had for a long time. Just before I left, I noticed that the gardener was thinning herbs and had them for sale, five dollars a pot. I bought some oregano and squeezed it into my milk crate, because I knew it would revive after I got it in my own garden, and that this would always remind me of this happy time.

My days were so packed on the scooter trip that I had to go back the next week to take the time to see the fort. The day I went was gloriously warm and sunny. It was not very crowded, due to COVID, and it suited me fine that there were few people.

Fort William Henry

Fort William Henry

In The Spy Who Loved Me, Viv praises "the stockade fort" in Lake George, which is, of course, Fort William Henry. I have often wondered whether Fleming knew the fort is a reconstruction. Fleming came from a land where half-timbered houses of Tudor times are still in use--I've even seen one housing a McDonald's. Viv's interest in Revolutionary War lore doesn't stop with the fort. She also mentions "Fenimore" Cooper (she leaves out the James) and is proud that her convent, back home in Montreal, owns the skull of Montcalm. I was startled when I read that last part, because I knew she was right: the Ursuline convent there does own that skull. I also knew who Montcalm was, which is pretty impressive for a seventeen-year-old.

I knew who Montcalm was, not because I live in the area and it was covered in school history class - I'm pretty sure it was covered but left my brain, frankly--but because my parents owned Barney Fowler's wonderful series of Adirondack Albums, which I had read by the time I was thirteen. Volume 2 (the green one) had a haunting story about an elderly nun remembering, historians take note, where Montcalm had been buried, having witnessed this as a little girl. She walked them to the spot in the convent, saying, "It rests here." That she had been present, which is disturbing, that she grew up to be a nun in that very convent, that she remembered accurately the location, were all fascinating to me.

I also had a love of Montcalm and of the fort because I was in the opera version of The Last of the Mohicans (composed by Alva Henderson) as a young teenager. Those were the days that Lake George Opera Festival, now called Opera Saratoga, performed at Queensbury High School, and recruited their supernumeraries from the locals. Were you aware there was an opera of The Last of the Mohicans? There have been nine movies, several TV movies, radio broadcasts, and plays, but the opera is an infrequently performed work--so infrequent that a quick Google of adaptations of the book might not even yield that there was an opera-- so I

Fort William Henry

was lucky to be a player in it. I doubt I'd ever have heard it if I hadn't performed in it; it is not easy to get a recording. My job in the opera was to be killed dramatically during the massacre, a job I loved, because a handsome man carried me across the stage before the gruesome part, and rehearsals meant that probably hundreds of times I was in his arms. It was the experience being at these rehearsals that I learned the significance of the local street names of Montcalm, Horicon, Mohican, and Uncas.

Also, in rehearsals, doing the same thing for hours, day after day, meant I got a pretty good understanding of the story, and developed a particular affection, historically speaking, for the Marquis de Montcalm, who was as merciful as you could possibly expect a victorious general to be, allowing the conquered to leave quietly, even permitting them to take their rifles with them.

In the opera version of The Last of the Mohicans, by the way, the title character is a Mohican, not a white guy who likes them a lot. I remember being puzzled when the posters came out and Daniel Day-Lewis was on them, and hearing the buzz that Hawkeye was the title character, not

Uncas. I also remember the entire audience erupting in laughter at one scene. In The movie, Cora and Alice and Uncas and Hawkeye, canoeing at top speed, are trying to escape Magua, and Hawkeye says, "Head for the river!" I read somewhere that it would take four days to carry a canoe from the southernmost part of Lake George to the most easily accessible part of the Hudson. In any case, the whole audience that day evidently knew that Lake George does not spill conveniently into any river, and I can still hear the laughter in my brain. Some of us discussed it later and were jealous of the waterfall in the movie, though. When you finally do get to the Hudson, the waterfall near Cooper's Cave is only about thirty-five feet, not the seventy-five or one hundred in the movie.

As far as I know, Ian Fleming was in Montreal infrequently, so where and why he picked up the factoid about Moncalm's skull being there I do not know, but it does add a level of intriguing knowledge to the narrative: the heroine is in the location Montcalm did something important. Her childhood involved knowing that Montcalm was historically important. Fort William Henry has had a much longer life as a tourist attraction than it did as a military stronghold. It's also been more successful. The original fort was built in 1755 by the English to hold that section of what they called the New World against the French. This gets confusing to school children because this part of history, called the French and Indian Wars, has New York State children rooting for the English, but just a few years later, during the Revolutionary War, the English are the bad guys. In any case, the fort was only about two years old when the pivotal Battle of Lake George occurred. Fort William Henry was defended by a skilled soldier, Colonel George Munro, and he was savvy enough to know he'd need reinforcements against the French, who had not only a brilliant commander, but the allyship of the Native Americans we call the Iroquois.

I have recently learned that Iroquois is not the term the people used for themselves, and that their own word for themselves is Haudenosaunee. Munro sent a letter to General Daniel Webb at Fort Edward, a few days' march away, for reinforcements, but reinforcements never came. Webb, believing that the situation was hopeless anyway because of an incorrect report that Montcalm had eleven thousand forces, declined to send help, and Munro had to endure knowing, with each passing day, that there was less and less chance of success. If Munro knew he was doomed, Montcalm knew, as well, that his victory was inevitable.

Montcalm was smart, cultured, learned, handsome, pious, and short. He predicted accurately that England could not hold on to the colonies the way they were going. Montcalm continued his brilliant career until death at only forty-seven, two years after his victory at Fort William Henry, and was buried in the Ursuline convent in Montreal. Now, the reason I am going on so much about Montcalm is the paradox that this brilliant soldier and commander, this expert at efficient killing and getting other people to kill, was not a bloodthirsty man. It was enough, at least in this case, to get control of the fort. He didn't kill those he vanquished or take Munro as a military prisoner. He just ordered the English to leave the fort. It was not Montcalm's fault that the massacre occurred, that his native allies killed the sick, the wounded, and Munro. They had been promised war spoils. Some took prisoners, some just killed.

What happened next is fuzzy in public consciousness, and not because historians don't know what happened. It's fuzzy because when James Fenimore Cooper got hold of the story, it wasn't good enough for him, and he had to insert a love story between one of Munro's daughters and a Native American he named Uncas, and a daring escape to the Hudson and a spot now called Cooper's Cave. It breaks my heart every few years, when I have to explain to a tourist that yes, this is Cooper's Cave and it is real, but that most of the story in Last of the Mohicans is not real. No, wait, yes, the battle is real. Yes, the fort is real. No, not THAT fort, it is only a recreation. Cooper's Cave, which was definitely not called that during the Revolutionary War.

Cooper's "Cave" seems to be only a large crack in the limestone, at the falls. It is visible from a platform with historical markers that, as wearily as I, attempt to explain where history leaves off and Cooper does his thing. During my lifetime, there was an opportunity to actually climb

The waterfall was more impressive in the movie Last of the Mohicans than it is in real life.

Reenactors at Fort William Henry

into the cave, but that was determined to be unsafe and really the viewing area is a better idea. The Hudson is changeable, and the waters can come up so quickly, and even when the water is low the roar of the falls makes it so that if you did fall in the swirling river it is possible no one would hear your cry for help. (It breaks my heart, most years, in early summer, when there is a newspaper report of someone drowning in the river or in Lake George. In my almost sixty years of life, I have seldom read an account of a local drowning in these waters; the poor victim usually comes from downstate and presumably learned to swim in pools.)

The waterfall was more impressive in the movie Last of the Mohicans than it is in real life. While Montcalm had been generous in his terms of surrender, and while he tried to dissuade his native allies from violence, he could not afford to have the English fort there to be re-taken and used against his forces. After Munroe's defeat, the fort was burned, only two years after its completion. It was in the 1950s that businessmen bought the property to save it from development, and recreated the fort to the original specifications. So, when Fleming was in the area, reconning for The Spy Who Loved Me, he would have been viewing a "fort" only about ten years old. I doubt he would have been unaware of this fact, but believe he chose to leave the newness out for reasons of atmosphere.

Before you even enter the fort, there are historical markers, and little outbuildings. One building I remember from my childhood, marking an old cemetery, has undergone a big change. It used to be that the actual

skeletons of several of the fallen were on display, behind plexiglass, in this little building. This used to creep me out and draw me in, in equal measures, but I was glad when, in 1993 Maria Liston of Adirondack Community College (now SUNY Adirondack) and a crew of archeologists studied the skeletons but then took them away. Now, there are photographs and expository plaques and artifacts, but no actual bones to see there.

One small, impressive log structure holds a vending machine, all different kinds of sodas. I love

The Garrison Gardens at Fort William Henry   A dugout canoe

that. Across from this machine is a plaque that the governing body of Fort William Henry should consider replacing, no matter what it would cost. It refers to Native Americans as "hostile Red Indians." While I tried to see the fort as though for the first time, this proved difficult. I read all the historical markers and learned more about my beloved Montcalm, but nothing that contradicted my already high opinion. I read the history of the area, but between New York State education requirements and the opera I was in, this was mostly review. I thought I might go on the guided tour, and there was one already happening, so I joined in, but immersion in New York State history made it so that as entertaining as the young man was, he didn't give me insights.

A reminder is not necessarily bad. And watching other people learn is delightful. What were the requirements to serve at that fort? One was the possession of two opposing teeth. Just two. They were needed to make sure the soldiers could eat hard tack, and they were rare enough in that time and place that making two opposing teeth a requirement was something that had to be brought up. The children in the tour group were tickled and disgusted to learn this. The guide, somehow dashing in his bright red period coat, laughed the laugh of recognition. He'd heard the disgusted gasps before.

There was a reenactor there that day, a woodworker turning spindles with a foot powered lathe. He was an old man, and local, so I asked if he knew anything about Ian Fleming in the area, but he did not.

My favorite part of the fort, often overlooked, is the tiny garden. It had been sensibly located inside the walls, and it was someone's job within the fort to tend it. Both officers and enlisted men could have a garden for personal use and I wonder who got the pleasure of looking after a garden instead of doing some more martial thing. Or, was it another duty that the person had to do on top of everything else?

You can look over the ramparts of the fort and get a lovely view of the lake, of the steamboats, and of the battlefield. When I was a teen, it was a tradition to take "Senior Skip Day," go to Lake George, have a picnic, and play frisbee at Battlefield Park,

Father Jogues statue in Battlefield Park

so when I think of that area I think as much of happy early summer days as I do of war. I doubt we gave much thought, as teens with frisbees, to why that park was called "Battlefield." Truth is, though, I was too scared to skip school and I was at my desk studying for Regents when my friends were picnicking, but I smile at the thought of their bravery and sense of freedom, which I lacked.

Standing at the fort, I could see not only the battlefield, but the end of the bike trail which goes between Lake George and Glens Falls. This bike trail mostly follows where there used to be a railway between the two towns. This train was no longer running when Ian Fleming was writing The Spy Who Loved Me, kind of a sad thing because he loved trains and it would have been great to see his heroine making her escape that way.

I love the Warren County bike trail, which is a seven-mile paved Father Jogues statue in Battlefield Park path from Glens Falls to Lake George, and I particularly enjoy doing it on roller blades. Roller blades, at least the way I do this, are just a little slower than a bicycle, so the scents and sounds of the trail are even more available to you. I particularly love the smell, in late summer to autumn, when the pine trees drop their needles. When enough of them fall, you can use them to slide down a hill, they are so slick and soft. Fleming worked pine needles into his book. Bond had to make a dummy of himself to throw the bad guys off, and he was so proud of using the pine needles as the dummy's hair that he bragged to Viv about it in what I see as a childlike and endearing way.

Unseen from the ramparts of the fort are the statues at the end of the park, one commemorating the Battle of Lake George, and the other, farther up the hill, of St. Isaac Jogues, who named the lake Lac du St. Sacrament, probably about 1646. They are surrounded by iron fences, meant to keep the statues from being vandalized. Isaac Jogues lacks the tips of several fingers, but he has not been vandalized; he was made that way. The statue was constructed to resemble Jogues after he was tortured by the Native Americans who really wished he would mind his own business and stop proselytizing to them. He didn't stop and was martyred not long after by a different group of Native Americans. Legend says Jogues's murderer later converted to Catholicism.

I lingered on the ramparts of the fort, enjoying the breeze, enjoying the views of the boats taking turns leaving the dock and docking, of the gulls either gracefully swooping over the water or arguing over something in the sand. I envied the people brave enough to parasail, and was happy for the families on the beach, most going in the water but some just lying on towels on the sand. The sun shone brightly, releasing a pleasant scent from the old logs of the fort, and I enjoyed that for a while.

The exit is near the gift shop, and I went in, but as I don't need a souvenir of Lake George I ended the day happily not purchasing anything, although the little pastel pink bow and arrow sets were intriguing.

New friends on four wheels

Chapter 5

"People I Met"

Within a few miles of getting on the road, I had the most marvelous experience. A biker, a real motorcyclist coming the other way, lowered his left hand with his palm open. This, in case you had not heard, is the international sign of motorcycle brotherhood. Could it be true? Could the Kawasaki rider actually have acknowledged me on my little scooter?

Soon, it happened again. Another biker, on a real motorcycle, gave me the sign. I returned it and felt so validated. There are a great many people on motorcycles in the summer New friends on four wheels in the Adirondacks, so by and by I thought I might do it first. What would another biker do, if I started the sign? The next biker that I saw, I did the sign, and he returned it! I started to sit a little straighter on that scooter seat.

At Elizabethtown, I headed to a Stewart's Shop to get a quick bite and to use the bathroom before primitive tenting, and when I saw a bunch of beautiful Harleys parked outside, I parked next to them. I was very pleased with my joke, placing my Honda next to those massive, powerful, and beautiful machines. When the group came out of the shop, I sang out, "I fit right in!" and the leader said, "You DO fit in. You are on two wheels!" and offered to pose for a picture. I never felt I truly fit in with the big boys, but I did feel completely accepted.

Some of the meetings with people I met in planned meetings, and they, too, were meaningful. Months ahead of the trip, when I didn't know for sure I would even get to do the excursion, I had been in touch with the current owner of the old amusement park at Northway Exit 29,

Mo Ahmad and me with my husband's badge

The trio station ruins at Frontier Town

Frontier Town. I had loved it as a kid, as so many had, but it was not just my own nostalgia that made me want to go there. When my late husband was a teen, his first job was as a sheriff at Frontier Town, riding his company-owned horse through town to round up the teenaged, hired bad guys. I intended to give my husband's badge to the current owner, who was looking for artifacts for a display.

I had found Muhammad Ahmad (Mo) through a Frontier Town Facebook group. What an amazing world, where we can make these contacts without having to have a friend of a friend introduce us! I had never met the man, never even spoken to him on the phone, when I messaged him that I was almost at the site. Then my phone lost internet, which is a common occurrence in the Adirondacks, and I didn't know if he had gotten my message.

He had gotten my message, and was waiting for me, and we posed for a picture before I gave him my Mo Ahmad and me with my husband's badge husband's silver badge, engraved with his name. He told me all the plans he had for the building, showed me both the new construction and where he was trying to honor the old Frontier Town. I look forward to visiting when it is ready, visiting the site, and my husband's old badge.

Anne Marie from the Shamrock Inn

I had only been on the road about an hour and a half by the time I got to Frontier Town, but I was tired, and Muhammad gave me free rein of the remains of the park. Not much is left but the A-frame that used to be the entry and the Frontier Town Train Station. It was oddly peaceful, surrounded by the most beautiful wildflowers, lightly scented and vividly colored even before the sun was bright. I sat in a sunny part of the station, because it was still a bit chilly in the morning, and listened to the birds sing for a while before I thanked my The train station ruins at Frontier host and headed north. Town Have you ever felt you should have met a person long ago? That was what it was like, talking to Anne Marie, the owner of the Shamrock Inn in Peru. If there is one person who sympathized with my crazy James Bond trip more than anyone, it is Anne Marie.

Her youthful good looks and zest for life make me think of Jamie Lee Curtis, and she has beautiful manners and exquisite taste in decorating. Each of her cabins was decorated and arranged to be at once completely usable and comfortingly beautiful. Anne Marie looked over the Pan copy of The Spy Who Loved Me, the one with the map of the Adirondacks on the cover and exclaimed that she loved the idea of redoing the trip.

Like me, she's a parent of an almost grown-up daughter and used to making more decisions for responsibility than Anne Marie from the Shamrock Inn for fun, and she was delighted on my behalf that I could have this adventure. Most of the cabins, thank goodness, have been renovated since she purchased the business, but one or two still had their 1950s wall coverings and bathrooms, and she generously opened those up for me to take a look. Anne Marie also posed for a picture on my scooter, packed me banana muffins for the road, and instructed me to call her if I had any troubles on the way. I sincerely believe that she would have dropped anything, night or day, to help me if I were in trouble. Her energy and enthusiasm was evident in every cabin, every square foot inside and out. Anne Marie had been a dentist before she "retired" to own a motel. I bet her patients had the most beautiful, perfect smiles.

At one point during my reconnaissance trip, I thought finding motor hotels would be easy. However, after finding the Shamrock, every one of the next few motels whose lot I pulled into was full on the following Saturday night. Finally, tired and discouraged, I decided to get lunch, still trying only to eat at places that had existed in Viv's time period, or were at least independently owned establishments. In Elizabethtown, about halfway between the Canadian border and Glens Falls, I found a restaurant and hotel called, interestingly, "Halfway House." On the porch was a man on his cell phone whom I took to be the owner. "No, we don't have anything. We don't have any room until October," he said, "You should have called earlier." Then a pause. "Steve. My name is Steve. You can try again next week but I don't think we'll have anything." I went into the restaurant, and soon enough the owner, a big, muscular man, came to take my order. "What can I get you?" he said. Channeling my best Sir Roger Moore, I said, "Information, Steve. I need a place to stay next Saturday." "We got a hotel right here." "Yes, but I just heard you tell somebody you are full. That's OK, though, you are in the business. You must know someone who's got some room. I don't mind tenting =" (now I was winging it) "- I just need a place to sleep." Steve said he had a friend with a primitive (no electricity and no water) campground, and when I said that was fine, he said, "Well, why don't you just pitch your tent behind the hotel? I have a nice clearing down by the river." I immediately said yes. I was so grateful. I brought out my Pan copy of The Spy Who Loved Me again, and explained about my scooter trip, and when I said "scooter" he got his wife to listen, because it turned out that Steve's wife also drove a Honda scooter. She was intrigued by the trip and happy to let me sleep by the river.

It was at that moment that I realized I had just committed myself to packing a tent in a scooter with only a milk crate for storage. I thanked Steve and his wife and happily, if nervously, headed home, telling my hosts I would see them Saturday afternoon.

And I did see them the next week, but only long enough to give them zucchini from my garden and to thank them for letting me stay there.

I am thankful I met Steve and his wife. Adirondack lodgings are expensive when you can even find them, and they charged me nothing to let me stay on their beautiful riverbank. The field by the river was so abuzz with bees that it was impossible to believe, while in the midst of them, that there could possibly be anything posing danger to the worldwide bee population. Bathing in the river was delightful. Sitting under the stars from nightfall until bedtime, and then with only a play tent between me and the outdoors, was miraculous to me.

I had not done primitive camping since my teenaged daughter was born, and there was a part of me that had begun to doubt I could ever do it again. Their generosity brought a part of me alive I thought was gone.

While Muhammad and Anne Marie made my heart warm, the truth is I was a little intimidated by both Steve and his wife. There is nothing in what they said to me that accounts for my being intimidated and I can't explain it. I am very grateful for their help and yet, I just don't feel the joy in writing about them that I do with other people. But the joy in the experience is unmeasurable.

My scooter trip through the Adirondacks was my first ever trip to Ausable Chasm, and it was magnificent. Ausable Chasm, "the Grand Canyon of the East" is a wonder of a river that has

Rappelling on the cliffs at Ausable Chasm

cut through miles of rock., with skilled, talkative guides who paddled the boats with just a little help from the guests. My guide, Owen, had just the right amount of knowledge and of sass in his banter. In my boat were two of the most charming children I have ever seen, preschoolers both, Tillie and Hugo, whose enthusiasm and wonder at the waters nevertheless did not make them lean over so far as to worry their careful dad. They were a beautiful family. "Okay, you'll see we have extra paddles; some of you may have to help out if we get stuck." I hoped that would not be me, because I was afraid of messing it up, but Hugo and Tillie became excited at the idea of helping, "And remember to keep your hands IN THE BOAT," said Owen as the children reached for the water, "Because sometimes we hit the rocks." And then we did, but Tilly and Hugo had their hands in the boat.

He told a story of a movie being filmed at the chasm, and the director needing a man to go over a cliff on a horse and into the water. So what did the producers do to find someone willing to go over a cliff? "Naturally, they went down to the nearest bar. And they found one." Hearing several of those in the boat gasp, Owen assured us that the horse was fine, and that the unwitting "actor" was not badly hurt. Owen seemed to be only a teenager and I am impressed with his poise, knowledge, and compassion. It was mostly a calm, very relaxing tour, with just a few rapid areas. Before we approached these, Owen would warn us, and tell the people with paddles (not me!) exactly what to do. Mostly the water carried us with just a little help in steering from Owen. Behind us, and sometimes in front of us, somehow evoking a hummingbird on water, another guide in a minuscule boat flitted from one tour group to another, making sure no one was in trouble. As we got to a broader part of the river, people in tubes floated just ahead of us or just behind us, and their contented expressions told me that the water temperature was relaxingly cool on this hot day.

It felt lovely to be in a group, and in the company of those charming children. I had been by myself mostly for two days, mostly just driving the scooter, and the children's happy laughter and the delight they had in the beauty they saw were contagious. They both had big brown, curious eyes, and Tilly's shiny black ringlets bounced as she talked. I do not think the children were twins, but from their manners and closeness, they might have been. When they saw the group rappelling from a cliff so high I couldn't even estimate it, they asked their dad if they could try this and his slow dry response, "Maybe later," made me think of exasperated parents all over the world.

I'd love to know whether Ausable Chasm has an intense training program or whether I just got lucky, but Owen was the perfect guide. He had just enough stories, just enough times of quiet when we could enjoy the sky and the water. He also knew how to make a dull story have a happy ending, and how to make us feel like we were a working team, even though we'd just met and would likely never see one another again.

The last night of my trip I stayed at Wiawaka Center for Women. By this time I was conflicted. I couldn't make up my mind whether I wanted, for the rest of my life, to only wear the one of two outfits I had that was clean, or to get home as fast as I can and have a choice of wardrobe, whether I wanted to be on the road more or never again. Yet I was sure of two things: I was looking forward to a hot shower and a real, cooked meal. I had had only one of those in four days, breakfast in Pottersville. The rest of the time I mostly ate my packed granola bars and fruit or stopped for a snack at a Stewart's or some Adirondack convenience store.

I was eager for my shower when I got to Wiawaka, completely focused on it, and when the woman in the room across from mine invited me to join her at dinner, I realized that I didn't want to have dinner in company. I had mostly been by myself for these past few days, seeing people only in small doses, and it occurred to me that this suited me fine. However, not wanting to appear rude, I said I would see her down at the main building, Fuller House, right at six. I didn't regret it.

There's a movie called Calendar Girls, where women of a certain age gather for "enlightenment, friendship, and fun," in their Women's Institute. They also pose nude for a calendar to raise money, but that's another story. Or maybe it's not: what greater act of sisterhood could there be than to raise money any way you can to help others?

It is refreshing, in Calendar Girls, to see women doing ordinary things and being seen as relevant. No Calendar Girls woman is seen as trying to make an identity through her posing; it is just a means to an end, and we see the women in their rich everyday lives. They run a flower shop, play the organ at church, play golf, care for family members and the movie shows these things as legitimate ways for women to use their time. This is mind blowing and validating in a world where movie dialog is given to men seventy percent of the time, and screen time is dominated by men. I found this Wiawaka group to have a Calendar Girls vibe, and by this I mean women who were quite aware of their relevance and living fulfilling lives and those lives included getting energy and validation in the company of other women. It was both empowering and comforting to be in this group.

Mostly these women are part of a book club, and I was more than accepted as one of them. These wonderful women asked all the questions about The Spy Who Loved Me that I had ever hoped anyone would ask. When they learned I had been an extra in the Joey King film Radium Girls, which filmed at Wiawaka, again they wanted to know all about it. Mostly teachers, but also writers, all told wonderful stories of their own lives. Several women shared their career stories. One woman told of her teen years, her family having to move, and that this meant leaving her "steady boyfriend." "Steady boyfriend," said another, "Isn't it interesting that girls these days don't get to date around and THEN go steady?" "Yes," said another, "It's sad. As soon as they go out with one, the girls are expected to drop everyone else. We had it better." We then had a lively discussion about how dating has changed from our own teen years to our daughters'. And it felt as though our experiences were relevant, as though not just our dating years, long ago, but our conversation, now, was important. Far from being sorry I had dinner with this group, I made sure to have breakfast with them as well.

This was a group of curious, educated, compassionate, "out" feminists. I had the pleasure of the type of free speaking I have not had since college days. Politics, bodily autonomy, the economics of poverty they may not be topics that make your heart sing, but the opportunity to discuss them freely put a song in my heart.

As with Anne Marie at Shamrock Inn, I have made a point of keeping in touch with the women of the book club, and in fact have visiting these wonderful women at Wiawaka on my calendar.

I was warned by some, before the trip, what a dangerous thing it was to travel alone, a middle-aged woman on a slow scooter in some unfamiliar territory. I was told there might be terrible people, sexual predators, con men. I even had a friend who lives four states away who offered to come up on his own motorcycle and keep me company (read: safe), but the fact is that everyone

I met, and most of the people with whom I had small social interactions, were wonderful and supportive, and I am glad the naysayers were wrong.

One of the most interesting things about me is, paradoxically, that my face is dull. This is not modesty, but math. It started in High School that people would call me by other people's names. Sometimes they would (and still do) get irritated when I don't answer to the other person's name, and even in other countries, and sometimes in languages I don't yet speak, I get mistaken for other people. The mystery was solved when someone in a college make-up class measured my facial features and found that the sizes of my nose, mouth, and eyes, and the distances between them all, were as normal, as average, as it was possible for a person's face to be. Since then, I have looked upon my being confused with other people as a superpower, for two reasons. The first is that I can help people not miss their loved ones. Almost invariably I get mistaken for a dear friend who has not been seen for a long time, and I can talk with the person making the mistake and reduce the pain of loss. The other reason is that, since people think they know me, they tend to think of me favorably at first meeting. It's possible this is something that helps me stay safe.

Now, let me tell you about some of the challenges I did face.

Chapter 6

CHALLENGES, CHALLENGES

Such a small thing can make a big difference, in an instant your feelings

can go from content to frantic. It's always amazing to me how this can happen. Len, when he lent me the scooter, gave me the only key. Just the key, no key ring. The key was approximately the size of a standard car key, if a different shape. It was too dangerous to keep the key loose, for I would be sure to lose it. But I didn't want to put it on my own key ring, because I had no intention of bringing my car key with me on my trip. If I lost my car key, this would be a disaster, because my little used Mitsubishi Mirage, the economy car of economy cars, somehow was designed so that each key costs three hundred dollars to make. I have one, and my best friend has the other, and I can't afford to lose one in the nearly two hundred miles between my house and the Canadian border. I decided to put the scooter key on a new key ring.

We all collect them, don't we, as little trinkets at fairs or conferences? I have them with bottle openers, with tiny stuffed animals, with emblems for not for profits, but I wanted a big, bulky one that I could not lose, and I remembered I had the perfect choice.

I once had a friend who did leatherwork, and was in the habit of making key fobs and giving them as "no reason" gifts, but I had not used mine because it was so bulky. Mark had died unexpectedly a few months before the trip, and I had put him out of my mind with other bits of sadness. But he had always been supportive of my Bond work, so I tried to remember where I had put the key fob. When I found it, I was surprised to see a charm I had not remembered on it, a silver disc on which was written, "Follow your heart." Perfect.

"follow your heart"

My riding jacket was another gift, a sturdy leather number with deep pockets, but the pockets had no zippers. For this reason every time I stopped, I kept one hand in the pocket, as if to keep the key from jumping out, so worried was I that I would lose it. Naturally, when I was riding, I didn't worry about losing the key because it was in the ignition. And, as the miles continued, as I stopped and restarted and got used to what I was doing, I no longer kept my hand protectively on top of the key ring whenever I had to stop the scooter.

So you won't be surprised to learn what happened. It was on the way back, when I had safely taken the key out of the ignition, put same in the pocket and back into the ignition dozens of times. I had stopped in Schroon Lake, an unfamiliar town, where I know no one. It was a Sunday morning, and many businesses were closed, so it was a challenge for me to find a place to charge my phone. I walked around the town, admiring the lake in the morning but not immersing myself in appreciating the beauty as I was too interested in finding an outside outlet. I walked up and down the main drag of the Village of Schroon Lake in vain. Eventually I gave up

Sailboat on Schroon Lake, from the gazebo

Sailboat on Schroon Lake, from the gazebo on that search and decided to take a hard roll from Stewart's down to the huge gazebo that looks over the lake. Stewart's uses real butter on their rolls and a fresh coffee and soft buttered roll always seems like an indulgent treat to me.

The Schroon Lake gazebo has two stories and a bathroom, and, to my surprise, electrical outlets, but no furniture, so I sat down on the concrete next to my charging cord. While I ate my roll, I enjoyed the morning breeze and admired the sailboats taking advantage of it. I watched a woman and her dog enjoying a morning by the water, sometimes playing fetch, sometimes just walking together and getting their feet wet.

After a while, my phone was charged up to a decent level, and I was relaxed and ready to get going on the road. I left the gazebo a bit reluctantly, because it had felt so good to be there, but it was time. I got on the scooter, moved it forward to release the brake, and put my hand in my pocket to get the key fob.

The scooter key was not there.

The key fob had not fallen out of my zipperless pocket, but the key was not on the ring. And there I was, alone in Schroon Lake. There I was, alone, having walked as far as I could in the village in search of a place to charge my phone.

What could I do? I had the phone charged to call someone, but whom would I call? The key I could not find was the only key to the scooter. It was a fifteen-year-old machine, and the key would not be in stock. And it was early morning, whom would I call, anyway? I hadn't heard the key fall, could not figure out how I could have lost it, but walked up and down the street, all around the gazebo, up and down the gazebo stairs, anyway, hoping to see that key. I took some comfort from knowing the key would not be stolen. It was no good to anyone else, and if someone had it and recognized it for a scooter key, that person would have already thought of trying to start the scooter, which was right where I had left it.

It was after what would have been a pleasant walk, had I not been frantically searching for my key, that I put my hands in my pockets again, and there the silly thing was. It had escaped from the key ring but had been in my pocket the whole time. It was kind of anticlimactic to fasten the key more securely, shake my head at myself, and start off again.

The challenge of packing

Packing was a challenge on my little scooter trip, a greater challenge for me, I think, than for the person I was copying. In the book The Spy Who Loved Me, Vivienne Michel has a scooter with saddle bags, that is to say, two storage areas, plus the area below the Vespa's seat. My borrowed scooter came with no saddle bags, only a milk crate on the back of the scooter. I gave some thought to buying saddle bags for the trip, but it turns out that would not be possible. First, they are not a standard item covered by Sportline and if I ordered them, they would not come in time, and second, as it turns out the milk crate was bolted on to the back of the scooter. I couldn't figure out how to take it off if I tried, and of course I would not make such a change to a scooter that I had only borrowed. So, I had to figure out how to pack the clothes and food for four days of travel in the gallon-sized area below the scooter seat and the standard milk crate on the back.

I'll confess I got in my own way, because on my recon I had told the owner of one hotel I would bring her tomatoes from my garden as a hostess gift, and those took valuable space. I had some nice green tomatoes ready to go, green because they would travel better. I added

My beautiful, tent, without, then with, "rain fly," by the river

zucchini and hoped the bumps and jolts of the road would not cause bruising. I put the vegetables under the seat. I put all the travel food, the map, the bug spray and sunscreen, all the things I would need in a hurry, under the seat.

How was I going to pack clothes for four days in a milk crate? Clothes, and a tent for heaven's sake. I'd saved money--heck, I'd made the trip possible--by planning to tent outside a hotel when there were no rooms to be had anywhere along my route. But how in the world would I fit all that stuff in that little space?

I am still so grateful for my sponsors. I realized that this was exactly what sponsorship was for, to get the right equipment. I ran out to a sporting goods store and found two quick dry t-shirts. I could rinse one out, while wearing the next. In addition, identical shirts would look better in the videos I posted on the way. I would always look the same, so if I needed to go back and retake a video, the images would look consistent.

In August, t-shirts would be appropriate, but Adirondack mornings can be chilly, so I packed a sweater, actually a "jumper" because I got it in a charity shop in Liverpool, England, where they don't use the word "sweater.". Of scratchy wool and a weird burnt orange, it is not pretty but is both light and warm. I would layer with this when cold but hoped not to take pictures in it.

My underwear was quick-dry, as was my bathing suit, and the bulkiest piece of clothing I would need, that leather riding jacket, would be on my back most of the time. My leggings, alas, were not quick dry, so I planned that they would just not be washed.

It was after I had made the plans to tent that I remembered the only tent I owned was a four-person. All right. Once again, I was grateful for my sponsors, and went back to the store for the smallest tent I could possibly find. This is when, for one of the few times in my life, I became grateful that I am short. I found a kid's play tent that was five feet long. I am five feet, three inches tall, so sleeping diagonally, I would just fit. A play tent would be fine for an Adirondack summer night, but as play tents don't have rain flies, I bought a plastic tablecloth to act as one. The tent had its own bag, so I draped the tablecloth over everything in the milk crate to keep things from flying off. It was not the most luxurious trip I had ever taken, but I felt satisfied that I had been resourceful and complete when I stood back and admired my packing job.

Chapter 7

Coming Home

It was a beautiful day when I had to return the scooter to its generous, kind owner. What a long way I had come! When I turned the key in the ignition, it was late afternoon, almost rush hour, and I went through intersections without fear. There was nothing I could do to adequately thank my benefactor. He didn't want money or recognition, and his garden had the same things mine did.

I can only say, here, that he is the best of the most generous hearts there are, someone who can provide a thing another person wants without payment or strings attached. The world has these people. I am lucky to know him.

I remember everything about the beginning of the trip, because being on the scooter was such a big deal, the trip so momentous, the responsibility so great. I remember approaching specific intersections with fear, hoping I stopped correctly, hoping I remembered to signal. By the time I was to return the scooter to its owner, riding was so familiar that my memories are more hazy. I know I went over the Route 9 bridge that showed our tiny waterfall on one side and Cooper's Cave on the other, but I don't remember it at all. Such things as traffic and bridges were no longer frightening to me.

Adirondack chairs in Lake George village

The scooter lives at a house in Fort Edward, a small, picturesque town, so I got the pleasure of leaving Route 9 and going through areas of old and regal trees, past a canal, past farm fields, and as I got closer I felt more and more that I didn't want to give the thing up.

I felt the air on my face for the last time on this machine that had served me so well, and thought, once again, about my original goals:

Could the fictitious Viv have made this trip? Had Ian Fleming made such a trip himself, as research?

The first was easy. I had made an educated guess that the trip was possible, but made this trek knowing that no educated guess is as good as real research, and I was prepared for surprises. Surprises I had few, but there remained some questions. How did our fictitious friend do laundry? Where did she use the bathroom when Stewart's shops had not yet been invented? The only answer is that Ian Fleming didn't think these things through.

Viv said it took her two weeks to get from the Canadian border to Lake George, and that it took her so long because she stopped at every tourist attraction. It possibly could have taken her two weeks--but not in October. Most of the attractions I visited closed at the end of summer, by Labor Day at the latest. Storytown, U.S.A., now the Great Escape, is now open in October, but only on weekends and only for the Halloween attraction called Frightfest. There would be very few tourist attractions anywhere on Route 9 for our heroine to have seen had she really done this trip in the autumn. I had only the time I had taken off from work, so at some sites I had rushed, but even if I took a full day at every major attraction, there's no way there were as many as to take a full two weeks to see them.

Viv might have extended her adventure by hiking, because summiting some mountains can take days, but she does not describe this, and, in any case, would not have had the room for the wool and the boots and the food and the tent that good hiking requires.

Lake George, the village, would not have been at its vivacious best in the fall. It was the crowding, the tourist traps, the crazy life of a north country August that Viv described. It was the thunderstorms of summer, not the nasty cold rain of the fall, that she experienced. Ian must have visited Lake George in the summer and put the liveliness of summer in his book, forgetting, when writing some descriptions, that his book took place in autumn.

I also have to conclude, albeit sadly, that Ian Fleming could not have made this trip for research. He surely went down this route at one point or another during the war years. The Northway not having yet been built except in small parts, Route 9 was the main route all the way from the Canadian border to New York City. Routes 22 and 9L follow the lake in parts, but Route 9 was the main route, the one he would have taken going from Montreal to New York during his career in intelligence.

Even for summer, and Ian was in northern New York for many of them, the descriptions of the outdoors are not very good, as if, when he was in the North Country, it was limited primarily to the house of his friends and the entertainment they gave him as their guest.

I knew even before I began that Fleming had most of his description for Lake George and Glens Falls, not really describing other areas. He mentions just Lake George attractions by name, and he falls down hard in describing specific Adirondack animals and terrain. I had the thought that perhaps there was not a lot to see, just trees, north and to the border, that paucity of things to describe had led to his not describing the area north of Lake George. But I was wrong about that. I was very wrong. Fleming gives such good descriptions of Lake George attractions, and so little of anything else when there is lots to see that I have to conclude that he simply never ventured further north than that village, at least not when he had a notebook at the ready.

Why am I so certain of this? It is because the Adirondacks are replete with one thing Ian Fleming could not resist describing: Birds. Magnificent birds. Slow-moving, immense herons, darting sparrows, regal hawks, flocks of gobbling wild turkeys, squawking gulls, all with personalities and plumage and all easily seen even from a moving motor scooter. In the book, Viv mentions chipmunks and deer, but the non-avian wildlife I saw were many more: snakes, porcupines, possums, and woodchucks in addition to the deer and chipmunks. The Fleming who spent pages describing a Jamaican "Doctor birds" would surely have mentioned the grandeur of a Great Blue Heron if he had ever seen one. Ian tries to cover for this lack of description by having Viv say she doesn't give a lot of description because she was not writing a travelog, but that does not really work for the character. She gives so much description to so many things she sees and thinks about that the lack of detail on the journey itself doesn't ring true. It feels like a kid who didn't really read the book trying to do a book report. I loved retracing Viv's adventure. I set out to learn, but I didn't anticipate the absolute delight it would be to scooter along the winding road, seeing so many animals and lakes and different varieties of plants. If I could do it again, I would, and I'd do it better, by which I mean I'd plan what I saw with more thought I'd give myself more time to see bigger sites such as Ausable Marsh. But if I did this again, I could never re-experience the mind-blowing delight of seeing things for the first time. Then again, now that I know this trip is possible, I also know the best, most enjoyable way to see the Adirondacks is by scooter.

Why didn't some researcher recreate Viv's journey sooner? After all, the most tenuous connection to James Bond garners visitors. I have recently been on a Bond tour where the guide said, pretty much, "Here at this patch of weeds used to stand a building where they filmed fifteen seconds of Thunderball," and everyone nodded reverentially and took photos.

With The Spy Who Loved Me, you can do so much more, such as drive the exact roads Viv would have taken and sip Maxwell House coffee in an authentic Adirondack cabin.

One difference is that most James Bond experts are English. They would not realize that so many of The Spy Who Loved Me sites are real, or that the area rivals any site in the world for beauty. It can be a burden to make any research trip, but particularly to go from England to remote northern New York State, without expecting a payback in terms of insight probably has never seemed worth it before. Briefly, they don't know what they were missing. Also it is notable that the book was never made into a movie, and movie sites resonate deeply and differently from book sites. Baker Street and Platform 9 3/4 are powerful tourist attractions that reference books, but would they attract as much attention without their movies? I think not. Then again, why didn't I do this before? Certainly the reasons other scholars didn't recreate this trip didn't apply to me. For me, the reason I didn't explore these sites before is an inverse of why other scholars did not: while other scholars may not even know the reality of the The Spy Who Loved Me sites, for me they are so real as to be mundane. I'm a half block away from Route 9 as I type this. I passed a half dozen quaint Adirondack cabins as I drove around town doing errands this afternoon. There was, I figured, nothing for me to see. I was wrong about that. There was a lot to see, when I endeavored to see it from Viv's point of view, and moreover, there was a lot to share.

I set out for information, and I found it. I also found adventure, freedom, and beauty. Not bad for a scooter trip.

Acknowledgements

Biddulph, Edward, the first to offer me money to do this Blow, David, Post Star story Brandt, Michel--identifying planet Calderoni, Tony, motorcycle jacket Carlsen, Rosalie, continued indulgent support, photography skills Cork, John, support from the beginning Cross, Steve, free place to say Cull, Tom, discovering me and giving me a chance to write Daly, Andy Daly, Kathleen, general support and scooter transport Dryden, Alice, my future biking pal Doolittle, Will, Post Star story Dudley, L, constant support and insight Firuta, Gary, support and encouragement Gonya, Erica, who supplied me with so many articles on Ian that she began to call him "our boy" Herter, Solange, access to Black Hole Hollow Farm and inside stories on Ian Ihsan, ?? the hundreds of articles I needed to make this happen Kelly, Anne Marie, real support and delicious banana bread Lilly Library, staff at Nelson, Anne, nodding with interest whenever necessary and connection to the scooter Ooi, Jennifer, reminding me about Fulton History Reep, Michael, Undying love and support which has taken many forms Sherman, Matt, browbeating me til i get things done Sherman, Michael--intriguing lies and one or two things that were true Swallow, Ashlee, art Staff at Sportline, taking me seriously Warren County Historical Society Wiawaka, staff at

Index Words, People, Whatever

Adirondack History Museum, Adirondack Mountain Club, Adirondack Mountains, Muhammad Ahmad, Animal Land, Ausable Chasm, Ausable River, Boquet River, Bond, James Bond, Bryce, Ivor Bryce, Jo Cross, Steve Diamonds are Forever Eagles Elizabethtown Fire towers Fleming, Evelyn Fleming, Ian Fort William Henry Frontier Town Gaslight Village Great Escape Goldeneye Halfway House Herons Holmes, Sherlock Hudson River Hyde Collection Jamaica Keeseville Kelly, Anne Marie Lake Champlain Lake George, lake Lake George, village Lake George Steamboat Company Land of Make Believe Monaco, Arto Montreal Natural Stone Bridge and Caves Plattsburgh Pottersville Remington, Frederic Rouse's Point Route 9 Sagamore Saratoga (Springs) Sculpture garden Shamrock Inn Sportline Spy Who Loved Me, The Storytown, USA Thrilling Cities Trout River Underground Railroad Museum Vespa Vorreyer, Robert Washington, D.C., Wiawaka Whippoorwills Whitney, Marylou Wood, Charles YouTube

Sources, books Conant, Jennet, The Irregulars Fleming, Fergus, The Man with the Golden Typewriter Fleming, Ian, Diamonds Are Forever Fleming, Ian, The Spy Who Loved MeFowler, Barney, Adirondack Album Fowler, Barney, Adirondack Album Lycett, Andrew, Ian Fleming White, William Chapman, Adirondack Country

Sources, online That YouTube channel with the better name for Iroquois Adirondack Park Agency Googlemaps

Sources, Ephemera Ausable Chasm brochure, 2022 Lake George Steamboat brochure, 2022 Natural Stone Bridge and Caves print ad, 2022

www.ingramcontent.com/pod-product-compliance
Lightning Source LLC
Chambersburg PA
CBHW061212230426
43665CB00032B/2993